Transit of Venus
Poetry Exchange

•

Venustransit-Lyrik-Austausch

Hinemoana Baker

Ulrike Almut Sandig

Glenn Colquhoun

Uwe Kolbe

Brigitte Oleschinski

Chris Price

Victoria University Press

TE WHARE WĀNANGA O TE ŪPOKO O TE IKA A MĀUI

VICTORIA
UNIVERSITY OF WELLINGTON

VICTORIA UNIVERSITY PRESS
Victoria University of Wellington
PO Box 600 Wellington
http://vup.victoria.ac.nz

First published 2016

National Library of New Zealand Cataloguing-in-Publication Data

Baker, Hinemoana et al.
Transit of Venus / Hinemoana Baker et al.
ISBN 978-0-86473-979-7
I. Title.
NZ821.3—dc 23

Printed by Printlink, Wellington

Wie schön leucht' uns der Morgenstern.
—Philipp Nicolai, chorale (1597)

Me mātau ki te whetū, i mua i te kōkiri o te haere.
Before you set forth on a journey, be sure you know the stars.
—Whakataukī (Māori proverb)

I'm thinking of a challenge for us all. The star in the sky
has travelled all the way from home. Now follow that!
—Bill Manhire, 'Christmas'

Contents / Inhalt

Introduction

A transit of Venus across the Sun takes place when the planet Venus passes directly between the Sun and Earth. During a transit, Venus can be seen from Earth as a small black disk moving across the face of the Sun. The Transit of Venus has fascinated contemporaries since its discovery in 1639 and plays an important role in the history of Aotearoa/New Zealand.

In 1769 the Royal Society sent Captain James Cook on a voyage to observe the Transit of Venus in Tahiti, accompanied by botanists Joseph Banks and Daniel Solander and astronomer Charles Green. By observing the Transit from multiple locations on the globe, scientists hoped to be able to calculate the distance from the earth to the sun, which would in turn enable them to determine the size of the solar system.

Cook was also given secret instructions to sail onwards in the hope of finding the 'Great Unknown Southern Continent' (Terra Australis Incognita) and after leaving Tahiti he made landfall in Aotearoa/New Zealand. Following a violent clash with local Māori at Gisborne, Cook sailed up the coast to Tolaga Bay, where the first friendly contact between Māori and Europeans took place.

Nearly 250 years later, another transit provided the impetus for the Transit of Venus Forum at Tolaga Bay, which aimed to celebrate the dual heritage between Māori and European, and to begin planning a shared future, using science as a touchstone. As *Listener* journalist Anthony Byrt wrote at the time, 'the shape of our terrestrial lives in New Zealand and Australia is the direct result of men with telescopes searching the stars.'

The Transit of Venus on 6 June 2012 was the inspiration for an international, multi-layered poetry project. New Zealand's status as the Guest Country of Honour at the 2012 Frankfurt Book Fair was a good opportunity to realise it.

Einführung

Bei einem Venustransit stehen Sonne, Venus und Erde exakt in einer Linie. Die Venus wandert bei dieser Erscheinung als schwarzes Scheibchen über die Sonne. Der Venustransit hat seit seiner Entdeckung im Jahre 1639 immer wieder eine starke Faszination auf die Zeitgenossen ausgeübt.

1769 wurde Kapitän James Cook von der Royal Society nach Tahiti entsandt, um dort den Venustransit zu beobachten. Begleitet wurde er von den Botanikern Joseph Banks und Daniel Solander und dem Astronomen Charles Green. Die Beobachtung des Transits von verschiedenen Orten der Erde aus, sollte es ermöglichen, den Abstand der Erde zur Sonne zu ermitteln. Wissenschaftler erhofften sich dadurch wiederum, Größe des Sonnensystems bestimmen zu können.

Cook hatte außerdem geheime Anweisung, anschließend weiter zu segeln, in der Hoffnung den „großen unbekannten südlichen Kontinent" (Terra Australia Incognita) zu entdecken. Nachdem er Tahiti verlassen hatte, stieß er auf Land, Aotearoa/ Neuseeland. Nach einem gewaltsamen Aufeinandertreffen mit den einheimischen Māori in Gisborne segelte er die Küste entlang bis zur Tolaga Bay, wo es zum ersten friedlichen Kontakt zwischen Māori und Europäern kam.

Fast 250 Jahre später gibt ein anderer Venustransit den Anstoß für ein Forum in Tolaga Bay, welches des doppelten Vermächtnisses von Māori und Europäern gedenken sollte, mit den Wissenschaften als Prüfstein für den Beginn einer gemeinsamen Zukunft. Anthony Byrt, Journalist beim *New Zealand Listener*, schrieb dazu: „Der Grundstein unserer Existenz auf dem neuseeländischen und australischen Festland ist das direkte Ergebnis von Männern, die mit Teleskopen den Sternenhimmel absuchten."

Der Venustransit am 6. Juni 2012 gab auch die Inspiration zu einem internationalen, vielschichtigen Lyrikprojekt. Der

In June of that year the Goethe Institut brought German poets Uwe Kolbe, Brigitte Oleschinski and Ulrike Almut Sandig to Tolaga Bay on New Zealand's East Coast to experience the transit with the New Zealand poets Hinemoana Baker, Glenn Colquhoun and Chris Price, and to condense their experiences into poetry.

After a warm welcome from the local community, the sun broke through in time for the poets and other participants to observe the Transit from the reopened Tolaga Bay wharf (the longest wharf in the southern hemisphere). They also took part in an eco-restoration project to replant the foreshore with species that would have been there in Cook's day. Some of the seedlings came from plants Joseph Banks had collected and taken to be cultivated at the Royal Botanic Kew Gardens.

In Wellington, the six poets gave a public reading, visited the *Dark Sky* exhibition marking the Transit at the Adam Art Gallery, and visited the collections at Te Papa Tongarewa, the Museum of New Zealand.

In October the New Zealand poets travelled to Germany to meet their German colleagues in a reVERSible translation workshop at the Berlin Literaturwerkstatt. After translating a selection of one another's poems, the poets performed them in Berlin and at the Hamburg Museum of Ethnology, and finally the project, the poets and the translations were presented at the Frankfurt Book Fair.

The next transit of Venus will be not seen until 2117.

Chris Price
International Institute
of Modern Letters

Aurélie Maurin
Literaturwerkstatt Berlin

Ehrengastauftritt Neuseelands auf der Frankfurter Buchmesse 2012 eröffnete die Möglichkeit für dessen Umsetzung.

Im Juni lud das Goethe-Institut die deutschen LyrikerInnen Uwe Kolbe, Brigitte Oleschinski und Ulrike Almut Sandig nach Neuseeland ein, um dort den Venustransit gemeinsam mit den neuseeländischen DichterInnen Hinemoana Baker, Glenn Colquhoun und Chris Price zu erfahren und das Erlebte in poetischen Texten zu verdichten.

Nach einer herzlichen Willkommensfeier in Tolaga Bay stand die Sonne gerade richtig, dass die DichterInnen und andere Teilnehmende den Transit vom neuen Tolaga Bay Pier (dem längsten Pier in der südlichen Hemisphäre) aus beobachten konnten. Sie arbeiteten außerdem an einem Umweltsanierungsprojekt mit, durch das das Ufergebiet mit Pflanzenarten neu bepflanzt wurde, die zu Cooks Zeit dort zu finden waren. Sämlinge stammten von Pflanzen, die Joseph Banks bei der Entdeckung Neuseelands selbst gesammelt und an die Royal Botanic Kew Gardens zur Kultivierung übergeben hatte.

In Wellington veranstalteten die sechs DichterInnen eine öffentliche Lesung, besuchten die *Dark Sky* Ausstellung in der Adam Art Gallery und Te Papa Tongarewa, das Nationalmuseum von Neuseeland.

Im Oktober kamen dann die neuseeländischen DichterInnen zum Gegenbesuch nach Deutschland, um zusammen mit den Deutschen an einem VERSschmuggel-Workshop der Berliner Literaturwerkstatt teilzunehmen und die Gedichte der KollegInnen in die eigene Sprache zu übertragen. Das Projekt, die AutorInnen und die Übersetzungen wurden dann in Berlin und in Hamburg der Öffentlichkeit vorgestellt und zum Abschluss auf der Buchmesse in Frankfurt präsentiert.

Der nächste Venustransit wird übrigens erst wieder im Jahr 2117 zu beobachten sein.

Chris Price
International Institute
of Modern Letters

Aurélie Maurin
Literaturwerkstatt Berlin

Hinemoana Baker

Translations by Ulrike Almut Sandig

Taranga's song

i sleep with a stone, oh make a sound
of it   stone warms as I drift, soft
thudding distant   and dust clatters
on my outer metal shell   Fire of fingers,

Taranga don't cry just move into the water
and open your arms   gram of atmosphere
song book, glass plates   Taranga your hair
I will rise in you like a village   perfectly

shaking the family, stay in the chair   Taranga
be precise or we will not
follow you, scream sand, knees and palms
all songs in the shell   oh make a sound of it

sound it to Kōpū to Pareārau to Tāwera

stand, Taranga, and standupstand
chink of right breath and milk, income
of eels and the overnight moment   Taranga hair
is the best tears make me   a hammock

Tarangas Lied

mit einem Stein schlafe ich o mach daraus
einen Klang   er wärmt mich beim Treiben
er schlägt in der Ferne dumpf und leis auf   Staub klickert
auf meinen Muschelpanzer aus Metall   Fingerfeuer

nicht weinen Taranga geh nur ins Wasser
und mach deine Arme weit auf   Gramm Atmosphäre
Liederbuch Scheiben aus Glas   Taranga dein Haar
ganz wie ein Dorf werde ich in dir wachsen   grandios

die Familie erschüttern bleib einfach sitzen   Taranga
erklär dich oder wir folgen dir
nicht schrei Sand Knie und Hände schrei
alle Lieder in die Muschel hinein   o mach daraus einen Klang

blas ihn den Venusplaneten Kōpū und Tāwera
und auch dem Jupiter Pareārau zu

steh auf Taranga steh aufrecht
der Lichtspalt aus gutem Atem und Milch der Ertrag aus
dem Aalfang und dieser lange dunkle Moment Taranga Haare
sind die besten Tränen bind mir daraus   eine Schaukel

I'd rather be crossing the surface of the sun with you

Creaking, I fail to sink, twelve
tons of pig iron in my gut.
An envelope of orders
a restaurant menu
opens in his dry fingers

each edict directs me one
degree at a time. In your
presence I make the sound of
a tympani, a tattoo
needle, the musical stretch

of my elm, my pine, my white
oak and fir, tensioned from my
tops to my futtock shrouds, live
ballast crawling through me like
a bloodstream. I wish I were

the Earl of Pembroke again
dirty with riches for fires
and not the antecedent
of broads who turn up dripping
with clams and zebra mussels.

I'd rather be crossing the
surface of the sun with you.
But somewhere in the strings of
my hair, a small boy, a sharp
loblolly boy, calls out *land.*

viel lieber würd ich mit dir die Sonne durchkreuzen

statt endlich zu sinken, knarre ich nur.
zwölf Tonnen Eisenballast in meinem Bauch.
die Speisekarte, ein Umschlag mit Befehlen
geht in seinen trockenen Fingern auf

jeder Erlass bewegt mich um je
einen Grad. in eurer Gegenwart
mach ich Geräusche, als wär ich
nichts als ein Meißel, ein Kessel

als hätte wer an meiner Ulme und Kiefer
Weißeiche, Tanne, von meinen Spitzen
bis zu den Püttingswanten, Saiten gespannt.
bewegliches Gut durchkriecht mich, als wärs

ein Blutstrom. ich wünschte, ich wär
wieder Earl of Pembroke, dreckig
an schwarzen Schätzen fürs Feuer
und nicht der Vorgänger

der Bräute, die vor lauter Venus-
muscheln, Wandermuscheln triefen.
viel lieber würd ich mit dir
die Sonne durchkreuzen.

doch irgendwo in den Schnüren
meines Haars ruft ein kleiner Junge
der Loblolly Boy vom Schiffsdoktor
ein Junge mit guten Augen ruft: *Land.*

What the whale said

Firefly, I speak of breath, that fine
bead. How we effervesce.

Hush darling full-of-air, convenor,
sad captor, your bones and mine

are seashells shot
through with a tender jelly.

A rabbit in your look as I break
the brine, my flukes a black book

a mast in your mind
cross of the drowned.

I groan with fathoms.
You glimpse of ray,

I swallow
the volume of a lagoon.

Was der Wal gesagt hat

Glühwürmchen, vom Atem sprech ich, von
dieser feinen Perle. davon, wie wir schäumen.

still, du luftgefülltes Liebchen, Funktionär
du trauriger Fänger, deine Knochen und meine

sind mit zartem Gelee
durchlöcherte Muscheln.

ein Hase in deinem Blick, wenn ich die See
durchbreche, die Fluke ein schwarzes Buch

ein Schiffsmast in deinen Augen
Kreuz für die Ertrunkenen.

ich ächze tief unten
du flüchtiges Licht

ich schlucke
das Ausmaß einer Lagune.

Songs to Venus I: The great flyer

I opened the basket we'd brought for our picnic
The day was a haze of soft light off the river
I selected the fizz in the two litre bottle
The green plastic plates and the lightweight tin cups
My wife wore the sun hat she'd bought at the Warehouse
Our friends with their animal, a sodden retriever
Were emptying bags of their swimsuits and towels
Spring tūī and kererū swung through the branches of
Natives, exotics, occasional powerlines

Then in a moment the air pressed us down
That air from above was the weight of a deluge
A sound like a wingbeat unbearably loud
Made us cover our ears and cry out in chorus
We all turned our faces to see what above us
Was pushing us forward and onto the ground
Nobody thought of a phone or a camera
Though there must have been three on our blanket alone
The bright air was empty, the trees bent at nothing

Except for a flash of what seemed like a laser
Or sunstrike or Venus at dawn in the winter
But the glare was much greater, we squinted our eyes
All that we saw were the trees on the riverbanks
Bending in sequence as the Great Flyer flew
Folding as if they themselves were the wings
And the river would rise like an eel from its bed
And be borne from us through the thin air of the valley
A sheer twist of water returning us home.

Songs an die Venus I: Der große Flieger

ich öffnete den mitgebrachten Korb für das Picknick
der Tag war ein weiches Lichtgeflimmer vom Fluss her
ich nahm die Zweiliterflasche mit Sprudel heraus
die grünen Teller aus Plastik, die Becher aus leichtem Metall
meine Frau trug den neuen Sonnenhut aus dem Warehouse
und unsere Freunde mit ihrem Tier, einem faden Retriever
nahmen aus ihren Taschen Handtücher, Schwimmzeug
Frühlingstūī und Kererū schwangen sich durch die Zweige
der hiesigen und der exotischen Bäume
über Starkstromkabel, gelegentlich verteilt

dann plötzlich drückte die Luft uns zu Boden
diese Luft über uns, sie wog eine Sintflut, ein Geräusch
wie das Schlagen von Schwingen, unerträglich und laut
ließ uns die eigenen Ohren zuhalten und schreien im Chor
und wir hoben unsere Gesichter um zu erkennen
was über uns sei, was uns vornüber drückte zu Boden
keinem kam sein Telefon, kam seine Kamera in den Sinn
obgleich allein drei auf unserer Decke wohl lagen
die helle Luft war so leer, die Bäume, sie bückten sich vor nichts

als vor den Blitz von etwas, das ganz wie
Laserstrahl war oder Lichteinschlag oder Venus
im Morgendämmern im Winter, doch das Funkeln war stärker
wir kniffen die Augen zusammen und sichtbar waren
nur die Bäume am Ufer des Flusses, die einer
nach dem andern sich beugten und hoben
als der Große Flieger vorbeiflog, die Bäume, sie schlugen
als wären sie seine Flügel, als würde der Fluss
aalgleich von seinem Bett sich erheben
durch dünne Talluft getragen werden
als reiner Wirbel von Wasser – er trüge uns wieder nach Haus.

Songs to Venus II: Point of light

The light from the doorway blackened her wings
Venus reached luminous hands through my skin
She held with her hands the planet inside me
The pain in my ribcage played like a song

She was so much more than a bright point of light
She was so much more than a road trip encounter
So much more than a humanoid shape
She was so much more than a twitch in the wheat field

More than a skin sample, more than a wingspan
More than transmission or disbelief
She was more than a tube in the navel or penis
More than a translucent gel in the morning

More than a urinary tract abnormality
Lenticular saucer, dirigible almond
A chevron, a dome, ellipsoidal ball
Triangular, delta, teardrop, cigar

Conical, boomerang, flat-topped straw hat
She was so much more than a wrong or a right

Hinemoana Baker

Songs an die Venus II: Lichtpunkt

die Flügel gegen das Flurlicht ins Schwarze getaucht
griff Venus mit ihren phosphoreszierenden Händen
durch meine Haut, griff nach dem Planeten in mir
in meinem Brustkorb spielte Schmerz wie ein Lied

sie war so viel mehr als ein heller Lichtpunkt
sie war so viel mehr als eine Reisebekanntschaft
so viel mehr als eine menschliche Form. sie war
so viel mehr als ein Zucken im Feld voller Weizen

mehr noch als Hautprobe, eine Flügelspannweite
mehr noch als Sendung oder Unglaube
mehr noch als Kabel im Nabel oder im Glied
mehr noch als schillerndes Gel gegen Morgen

mehr noch als eine Harnwegsabnormität
Untertasse, linsenförmig, lenkbare Mandel
Winkel und Kuppel, elliptischer Ball
Dreieck und Delta, Träne, Zigarre

konisch, Bumerang, flacher Strohhut
so viel mehr war sie als ein Falsch oder Gut

Songs to Venus III: Kaikoura lights

Just down off Blenheim, Cape Campbell way, we joked
it was Rudolph out front, Father Christmas with his sleigh
but then this target moved towards the freight plane, the Argosy
and parallel-tracked it a good twenty miles, thirty perhaps.
The light and the aircraft at ninety degrees to each other at all times.
Then it happened again, when the TV were on board.
That's when it went global. *What you're about to see*
was not only witnessed by the five on the aircraft
but recorded on radar. And that's the thing.
They've said harbour lights reflected off the breasts
of mutton birds, unburned meteors, drug runners,
squid boats, it was Venus, it was Jupiter.
But no-one's explained how I can suddenly see
Venus and Jupiter doing a hundred and forty
knots on my radar. End of story.

Songs an die Venus III: Kaikoura Lichter

gleich hinter Blenheim, Cape Campbell Way, wir witzelten,
das wäre Rudolph da oben, der Weihnachtsmann mit seinem Schlitten.
aber dann bewegte sich das Ziel auf den Frachtflieger zu, die Argosy,
und flog mit ihm auf gleicher Höhe gut zwanzig Meilen, vielleicht dreißig.
Licht und Luftfahrzeug in neunzig Grad zueinander, die ganze Zeit.
als das Fernsehen an Bord war, passierte es wieder.
und da wurde es global. *Was Sie gleich sehen werden,*
haben nicht nur die Fünf hier im Flugzeug erlebt, es wurde
auch auf Radar aufgezeichnet. und das ist es ja gerade.
es wird behauptet, Hafenlichter hätten sich auf den Bäuchen
von Mutton Birds reflektiert, auf unverbrannten Meteoren,
auf Drogenkurieren, Kalmarenfängern, Venus war's
und Jupiter war's, aber keiner hat mir erklärt, wie ich plötzlich
Venus und Jupiter mit einhundervierzig Knoten
auf meinem Radar sehen kann. Ende der Geschichte.

dismantling the crane

What is silver? Into this finger-space
the kotuku appears, flying once only
and far – to Holland, the vacated

apartment of your quiet friends
beaded slippers for sale
behind the silhouette

of the Moroccan woman whose feet
have been hurting her all day.
What is lost, here, where there was not

even eye contact, not even
eyes? Here a woman floated half-
miserable above land clutching

a posy – now there are growing
flowers, red with fat, sappy
green stalks and spongy leaves

and beside them the neighbourly
buttercups. Silver has become
hammer and aluminium. The star

in her firmament makes her way
over Rarotonga murmuring
hoki mai, hoki mai . . .

Meanwhile, how can this tūī
be so violently black? White
petals could be made of

den Kran zu zerlegen

was ist silbern? zwischen meinen vier Fingern
taucht der Reiher Kotuku auf, er fliegt
ein einziges Mal nur und weit – nach Holland

zur geräumten Wohnstatt deiner stillen Freunde
mit Perlen besetzte Pantoffeln, zum Kauf
feilgeboten hinter dem Umriss

der marokkanischen Frau, deren Füße
schon den ganzen Tag wehtun.
was ging hier verschütt, wo's nicht

einmal Augenkontakt gab, nicht einmal
Augen? hier trieb eine Frau lächerlich
jämmerlich über das Land, in der Faust

ein Sträußlein mit Blumen – nun wachsen hier
rote Blüten, die mit den fetten, grün
saftigen Stengeln, den lappigen Blättern daran

und nebenan in guter Nachbarschaft
die Butterblumen. silbern sind heute
Hammer und Aluminium, der Stern

in seinem Firmament zieht über
Rarotonga hinweg, Armstrong's Island
und murmelt hoki mai, hoki mai . . .

wobei, wie kann der Honigfresser Tūī
hier nur so schrecklich schwarz sein?
sein weißes Federsträußlein könnte auch

icing sugar, he flutters his wattle
with his two voice boxes. I sit here
wearing my bottle top, my lips

the dome above me dewy
with condensation. Outside
men in orange vests prepare

to dismantle the crane
its four ropes of chain rise
like snakes from the bed

of a dusty truck, link after link
on and on
until the morning is over.

aus Puderzucker sein, er plustert die Gurgel
mit seinen zwei Kehlköpfen auf. ich aber sitze
mit meinem Kronkorken drauf, meinen Lippen

und über mir ein Gewölbe, taufeucht
von Kondensation. draußen rüsten
sich Männer in orangenen Westen

den Kran zu zerlegen
seine vier Ketten heben
sich wie Schlangen vom Boden

eines staubigen Trucks, Glied um Glied
weiter und weiter
und dann ist der Morgen vorbei.

The fifteen paces between my socks and my shoes

1

The hotel room is a yawning
cavern and I have forgotten my
carabiners. The bed's made
tight, the linen's cool, the overblanket
smells of soap and someone's

breath. You're in Ruapehu Street
between the ill-fitting
fitted winter sheets now bald
of any fleece. Yellow makes you scratch.
A planet is getting ready for its big moment.

2

These two boys have to jump a little
to see into this telescope.
You can't look directly at it, man.
Ka wreck koe i tō eyesight.
The transiteers, the singing politicians,

the old light of the new
nation. All of us stroll
along the revamped wharf
pitching our wishes
at the glinting Pacific.

And she's there too,
the one they call Holden Torana
or Skinny Banana, Madame Iguana.
She'll be long dead when they bring up the time
capsule. She'll leave her responsibilities

die fünfzehn Schritte zwischen meinen Strümpfen und meinen Schuhen

1

das Hotelzimmer ist eine gähnende
Höhle, ich hab meine Karabiner vergessen.
die Zudecke ist fest gesteckt, die Bettwäsche
kühl, der Überwurf riecht nach Seife und Atem

von einem Andern. du bist in der Ruapehu Street
zwischen schlecht gespannten Winterlaken, ganz
ohne Fütterung. von Gelb musst du dich kratzen.
ein Planet plant seinen großen Moment.

2

die zwei Jungen müssen hüpfen
um durch das Teleskop zu spähen.
Mann, du kannst nicht direkt hinsehen.
Ka kaputtmacht koe i tō Augen.
Transiteure, singende Politiker

das alte Licht der neuen
Nation. wir alle spazieren
den aufpolierten Kai entlang
und schleudern unsere Wünsche
dem schimmernden Pazifik entgegen.

und sie ist auch da
Holden Torana genannt oder
Skinny Banana, Madame Iguana.
sie wird längst tot sein, wenn die Zeit-
kapsel aufgemacht wird. sie wird

purring in their red
blankets. We will monitor
the spectrum of scattered
sunlight on her surface.
She will say, in her way:

parachutes are heritage seeds
parachutes are significant star systems
parachutes are priestesses dancing and dying

3

I wasn't here for Nukutaimemeha
therefore this is not the real globe.
The girl with the grass-green ring

was not here for Horouta and neither was
the Ginger Bee, nor the sailor singing his insistent songs
of icebirds and liquor. All things move South

when they become cold. All things move North
when they become cold. All things make sails
from the liquid ocean, from their lala language.

4

In eight minutes your light
will reach me, hāngi smoke in my mouth.
The light which fell on my newborn body is still alive.
I plant a tree at the mouth of the Uawa river
in your name my crawling, bawling space station.

It is imperative I be as far away from you as possible.
You rise from the yellow bed, black and cold
and travel four hours
every cent of you making war
the telescopes of the world trained upon you.

alle Zuständigkeiten fahren lassen
und in ihren roten Bettdecken
schnurren. wir werden das Spektrum
des gestreuten Sonnenlichts auf ihr
im Auge behalten. auf ihre Art wird sie sagen:

Fallschirme sind Sternensysteme
Fallschirme sind Samen voll Erbgut
Fallschirme sind sterbende Priesterinnen im Tanz

3

für Nukutaimemeha war ich nicht da.
darum ist das hier auch nicht der echte Erdball.
das Mädchen mit dem grasgrünen Ring

war für Horouta nicht da, ebenso wenig
war's Ginger Bee und auch nicht der singende Seemann
mit seinen ständigen Liedern von Eisvögeln und Schnaps. alles
    zieht südwärts

wenn es erkaltet. alles zieht nordwärts
wenn es erkaltet. alles schneidert sich Segel
aus flüssigem Meer, aus lirum larum language.

4

in acht Minuten wird dein Licht mich erreichen
mein Mund voller Rauch, voller Erde, voll Fleisch.
das Licht auf meinem neugeborenen Körper, es ist ja
immer noch da. an der Mündung des Flusses Uawa
pflanz ich einen Baum für dich, du meine
krabbelnde, babbelnde Raumstation.

es ist unumgänglich. ich muss so weit wie möglich
von dir weg sein. du steigst aus deinem gelben Bett
bist schwarz und kalt und vier Stunden unterwegs.
jeder Cent in dir führt Krieg
die Teleskope der ganzen Welt
sind auf dich gerichtet.

Ulrike Almut Sandig

Translations by Hinemoana Baker

es war für alles gesorgt. alle Gäste waren
erschienen: die Astrophysiker und Astronomen

von Rang, die Bildungsministerin und nicht
zu vergessen: die tätowierten Freunde der Sterne

es waren alle gekommen. man trug Brillen
aus Pappe und schaute gen Himmel, der Himmel

selbst hatte Platz freigemacht für den Durchflug
der Venus vor dem breiten Antlitz der Sonne.

es war für alles gesorgt. als erstes bemerkten
die tätowierten Freunde der Sterne, dass etwas nicht

stimmte. nach und nach fielen Forscher mit ein:
wo bleibt die Venus? wo bleibt der Schönheitsfleck

des Planeten auf unserem Sonnengesicht?
niemand sah nichts. lag es am Datum? lag es am

Licht? die Teleskope zeigten ihr Bild
vom Venustransit – mit den eigenen Augen

sah man es nicht. die Forscher legten die Stirnen
in Falten, die Bildungsministerin zweifelte

am Konzept. nur die tätowierten Freunde der
Sterne lachten sich krank und schnitten sich

langsam dunkle, runde Motive in ihre Gesichter.

it was all arranged. all the guests
had arrived: the distinguished astrophysicists

and astronomers, the minister of education and let's not
forget: the tattooed friends of the stars

everyone had come. they wore glasses
made of cardboard and looked to the sky, the sky

itself had made space for the Transit of Venus
across the sun's broad countenance.

it was all arranged. **the tattooed friends of the stars**
were the first to notice something

wasn't right. one by one the experts chimed in:
where's Venus? where's the beauty spot of

the planet on the face of our sun? no one saw
nothin'. was it the date? was it the light?

the telescopes showed their images
of the Venus transit – with the naked eye alone

you couldn't see it. the experts furrowed
their brows, the minister of education questioned

the planning. only the tattooed friends of the stars
laughed and laughed and carved slow,

dark, motifs on their faces.

alles muss ich zweimal sagen,
alles muss ich zweimal tun. alles

muss ich wiederholen: alle Fehler
und jeden Verrat, immer zweimal: TEST!

**TEST! ich bin ein zweistimmig singender
Vogel mit Menschengesicht**

und schwer als schräges Tier zu erkennen
wenn ich im Farnbaum sitze

und zweistimmig klirre, zweistimmig
klicker und mit dem Schnabel

knirsche und knarr. ich bin
eine Reisegesellschaft und lock dich

gen Süden, als läge das Glück
tatsächlich unterm Äquator begraben.

aber lass dich nicht täuschen! mir
ist nicht zu trauen oder wenn

dann immer nur zweimal. dir
ist nicht zu helfen, kein einziges Mal.

ich bin ein Teekesselchen auf zwei Beinen
und trage den schwarzen Talar

meines Vaters, seinen weißen Kragen
und die Mädchenträume meiner

I say everything twice,
do everything twice. I repeat

everything: each mistake
and every betrayal, always twice: TEST!

**TEST! I am a double-voiced bird
with a human face**

and it's hard to tell I'm an odd
bird at all, when I sit in the fern tree

and double-clink, double-
crunch and grind

and creak with my beak. I am
a travel company luring

you South, as if happiness
really is buried below the equator.

but don't be deceived! I can't
be trusted or if I can then

only twice. you can't be
helped, not even once.

I'm a little two-legged teapot
wearing my father's

black cassock, his white collar
and I carry with me

Mutter trag ich auch mit mir herum.
wenn ich dich verlasse, dann

immer zweimal:

einmal im Süden, aber das nur zum Test
und einmal STOPP! auf Nordwest.

my mother's girlhood dreams.
when I leave you, it's

always twice:

once in the South, just as a test
and once STOP! in the Northwest.

seit Tagen bewegt sich die Luft: die Bäume
schleudern sichtbare Pollen gegen die Augen der
Kalten Sophie und gegen den leeren Himmel
darin. sie zielen auf alles, was unsichtbar ist:
auf den Nachmittagsmond, die Satelliten im
Orbit und in ihren Forschungskapseln hinter
der Venus all die verschollenen Hunde und
Affen. in meinem Hof die Kastanie macht leise
Gebärden, die ich nicht versteh. wenn die Erde
sich dreht **und sie dreht & dreht sich ja immerzu!**
und Europa sich gerade unten befindet, dann
regnet es Fünffingerblätter in die Milchstraße
herein, und die Kastanie in meinem Hof holt
für ihren letzten entscheidenden Schlag aus,
den ich auch nicht versteh.

the air has been moving for days: the trees pitch visible pollen into the eyes of icy Saint Sophie and into the empty sky inside. they aim at every invisible thing: at the afternoon moon, at the satellites in orbit and all the missing dogs and monkeys trailing Venus in their space capsules. in my courtyard the chestnut makes quiet gestures I do not understand. when the earth turns (**and it does turn, turn, turn!**) and Europe finds itself underneath, then five-finger leaves rain into the milky way. it pulls back for its final decisive blow, which I do not understand either.

meine Liebe, die Spatzen pfeifen auch hier von den Dächern
dass alles, was da ist, sein Gegenteil hat.

    erst gestern sah ich eine zweite Ulrike
in die Kamera lachen, aber die sah mir überhaupt

nicht ähnlich, ich hab sie kaum wiedererkannt.
meine Liebe, du + ich + alles, was da ist

    wir könnten auch unser Gegenteil sein. ich könnte
ganz anders heißen. wie wäre es mit **Hinemoana?**

sieh her: selbst wenn ich mich gar nicht bewege
dreht sich der Globus immer

    immer im Kreis. wer hat auch behauptet
der Aufenthaltsort der Antarktis sei immer

immer ganz unten? ich war es nicht
Hinemoana war's nicht und du

    warst es auch nicht. breit und verletzlich
schiebt sich die Antarktis

der Bautzener Straße entgegen
+ ich muss jetzt schließen + bleibe

    deine Hinemoana. P.S.: nur die Spatzen finden ihr Gegenteil nicht.
die Spatzen sind immer die Spatzen

auch hier.

my love, it's spreading like wildfire here
too, so it's true, everything has its opposite.

> just yesterday I saw a second Hinemoana
> laughing into the camera but she didn't look

like me at all, I hardly recognised her.
my love, you + I + everything that exists

> we could all be our opposites. I could have
> a different name. how about **Ulrike?**

look: even if I don't move at all
the globe always turns

> always circles. who the hell said
> the Antarctic is always

always underneath? it wasn't me
it wasn't Ulrike and it wasn't

> you either. wide and fragile
> the Antarctic inches

towards Bautzener street
+ now I must close + remain

> your Ulrike. p.s. only wildfire can't find its
> opposite. wildfire is always wildfire

even here.

Against disappearance

This is an excerpt from 'Gegen Das Verschwinden', written two years after the Transit of Venus Poetry Exchange project. It is based on Ulrike Almut Sandig's research on the next transit, projected to occur in 2117.

2117–12–11, 11:45, I am reading in the projections. For the last 35 minutes, Venus has been tracking across the sun. But, my dear son, that's not what I am thinking about. In case you have ever asked yourself why I have taken your daughter to this distant archipelago then you are just about to find out. All along the landing jetty there are telescopes and their images are being projected onto a screen in front of the gentle waves of the Pacific. The little one is running from one to the other with a special pair of glasses made out of papier-mâché on her nose and is comparing the pictures in the eyepieces. Some of the telescopes are not working properly, the pictures are upside down. And we are wondering, even though we have no idea about astrophysics, which of the pictures is correct? Where exactly is Venus? Is it crossing in front of the upper or the lower half of the sun?

This morning I gave a talk on one of the festival stages on the beach. It was about – to cut a long story short – about the significance of Venus in the history of European poetry. I could have talked about the disappearance of the English language after the implosion of the US-American Empire or about the change to the genitive in the context of the shift in perceptions of property and belonging. These are all research areas more or less familiar to me, and which you, as a good son, may have picked up on in some way. I could also have spoken about baking recipes. Nobody was interested in my talk; I'll only admit that to you, not even to myself. For the festival organisers it was the contribution from the old world, so they had to invite me. For me it was nothing but a pretext for travelling here and now I'm going to tell you the reason why.

The other contributors were sitting on the long row of seats behind me: the Minister for Science and Culture with a glowing

green tattoo around her mouth and chin; a Russian astrophysicist with a nervous tic in her right foot, which set the stage floor moving imperceptibly; some faceless descendant of James Cook; the local mayor and a South African art photographer whose camera was clicking away behind me while I was giving my talk. The little one, dragging her tiger under her arm, was running round the edge of the stage and didn't look at us even once, but kept the closed sky above the bay in her vision. She was the one who first saw the rip in the cloud cover. We were just singing the national anthem as she stretched her arm up to the sky and called to me, 'The sun, the sun the beautiful sun is here!' But perhaps I am only imagining that she called out because everyone around me was singing with such vigour and I only saw her mouth move to form the shape of the word sun, three times, the rest is just a guess.

It is just before twelve. Venus is just a dark drop in front of the glowing orange disc of the sun, sometimes at the top, sometimes at the bottom, depending on the telescope you choose. You can't see anything with the naked eye. Nor with these protective glasses made of papier-mâché that we are all wearing with such seriousness. Everyone except your daughter who threw hers into the waves, saying that there was nothing there; that we were making it up. And wasn't she right? Couldn't it really be some sort of animation that is being projected onto a big screen, and the actual transit of Venus across the sun could have taken place long ago, on a different day altogether or in the night, protected from our view, or maybe it didn't happen at all.

The festival has finished. The first buses are arriving at the bay. The little one is standing by the pebble beach with her dress dripping. She is shading her eyes with one hand and looking at a dark grey military boat that is moored silently in the bay. I am just going to get her and put something dry on her. And then we will take one of the buses to Uawa, a little village not far along the coast from here. That's where it will get exciting, my dear son.

It's still Saturday afternoon, sometime around four. According to the telescopes, Venus has reached the outer rim of the sun's disc. And it looks as though I have found them. They are behind the last buildings in the village in a rainforest that muffles the sound of the South Pacific crashing on to the beach. They are surrounded by beech trees, climbing plants, light falling through the crowns of the tallest ferns.

My grandmother planted them a long time ago. To be precise: 105 years ago. Your great-grandmother. We have her name, you and I, and the little one too of course. It is quite a normal surname but of course in a place like this, where no one speaks our mother tongue, it sounds strange, even to me, when the compère says it and the amplifier throws it into the coastal air like one of those inflatable penguins that belong on a different coast, in a different story. Here our name is just like one of those inflatables, filled with air. No one who hears it thinks of the bare earth of the Erz Mountains, where nothing grows because the soil is poor. Sandy soil that gave one of our other ancestors – a poor farmer with thick eyebrows framing his tired eyes – his name. We don't know who he was. We don't think about him. We just have his name. But it is our name too, isn't it? I'm just thinking of the woman who planted the trees. I want to tell you about her.

There is a register of all the trees planted on Notonesia* and in it you can find listed each single tree planted since the beginning of the reforestation programme and next to it the name of the person or the institution responsible for planting it. I found your grandmother's name in the register. Don't ask me what she lost here. Perhaps the last transit of Venus? It took place in the year they started reforestation. I have no idea what made my grandmother come to this distant place to view it. But I found her trees. A little

---

* The name of the island state Notonesia goes back the ancient Greek *notos und nēsoi* and means 'southwestern islands'. Notonesia will be formed in the year 2062 out of the New Zealand we know today. The rising sea levels will mean that the number of islands will be much greater than today. The official languages will be Māori and Notonesian sign language. English will have declined into insignificance after the end of the US-American empire.

taupata with leaves like spectacle lenses, it's actually more of a bush than a tree but with thick clusters of flowers hanging from the trunk. And next to this bush there is a Tī Kōuka, and that is a real tree. It is tall and slender. Its leaves protrude into the early summer air as if they were nothing but an illusion, which could burst at any moment and be nothing but a memory. A biologist from round here helped me to find the trees, a man with delicate flower-like patterns on his face. He says that the little berries of the Tī Kōuka are eaten by what they call wood pigeons, an amazing bird with a big belly. Belly stuffed with darkness and little berries.

That's all that I have found, my dear son. You may think that it is far too little. It is probably nothing in comparison to all the important things that have happened to you in the last few years. Your daughter doesn't seem to be very interested either. She is back in Uawa where there is a tent the size of a hot-air balloon in which you can dance wildly and throw white balls into the air. She even let the biologist take her by the hand without protest. The two of them wandered off to the edge of the village past a paddock surrounded by a fence made of artificial wood. Two horses, a gray and a mare the colour of a fox, were standing there and looking as if they had been there 100 years ago, standing and looking. The little one and the biologist were walking away from me to the edge of the village and looked like father and child.

Translated by Peter Thompson

Glenn Colquhoun

Six Songs for Ernst Dieffenbach

Translations by Uwe Kolbe

On a Journey to Aotearoa, the Crew of the *Tory* Sing in Honour of the German Naturalist, Ernst Dieffenbach.

Dieffenbach, Dieffenbach, What sort'a Leakin' Ark?
What sort'a Leakin' Ark, Cutter or *Cutty Sark*?
Dieffenbach, Dieffenbach, Shivers your Creakin' Arse?
Heave Away, Haul Away, Heave Away, Ho.

Dieffenbach, Dieffenbach, What sort'a Heathen Art?
What sort'a Heathen Art, Measures the Tūī Fart?
Dieffenbach, Dieffenbach, Here's to the Inky Lark!
Heave Away, Haul Away, Heave Away, Ho.

Dieffenbach, Dieffenbach, King a' the Buttercup.
'Naki, Tabaccy, Greywacke and Fuck.
Dieffenbach, Dieffenbach, Jesus! The Clutter-Up!
Heave Away, Haul Away, Heave Away, Ho.

Dieffenbach, Dieffenbach, What sort a' Pākehā?
What sort a' Pākehā, Jack Tar or Bleedin' Heart?
Dieffenbach, Dieffenbach, Heigh-ho, the Patriarch!
Heave Away, Haul Away, Heave Away, Ho.
Heave Away, Haul Away, Heave Away, Ho.

Auf der Reise nach Aotearoa, gesungen von der Mannschaft der *Tory* zu Ehren des deutschen Naturforschers Ernst Dieffenbach.

Dieffenbach, Dieffenbach, hat diese Arche 'n Leck?
Hat diese Arche 'n Leck, Cutty Sark ohne Heck?
Dieffenbach, Dieffenbach, geht dir dein Arsch im Dreck?
Hiev dich was, ziehe ab, hiev dich was, ho.

Dieffenbach, Dieffenbach, bist was 'n Heidenschnurz!
Bist was 'n Heidenschnurz, misst noch dem Tūī sein Furz!
Dieffenbach, Dieffenbach, der's mit der Tinte tut!
Hiev dich was, ziehe ab, hiev dich was, ho.

Dieffenbach, Dieffenbach, Butterblumen abgerissen!
'Naki und Knaster, Grauwacke, beschissen.
Dieffenbach, Dieffenbach, Jesus! Alles verschmissen!
Hiev dich was, ziehe ab, hiev dich was, ho.

Dieffenbach, Dieffenbach, bist was 'n Pakeha?
Bist was 'n Pakeha, 'n Jack Tar oder 'n Opapa?
Dieffenbach, Dieffenbach, Hey ho, großer Star!
Hiev dich was, ziehe ab, hiev dich was, ho.
Hiev dich was, ziehe ab, hiev dich was, ho.

On the Upper Slopes of Mt Taranaki, Ernst Dieffenbach Considers the Korikori (Also Known as the Mountain Buttercup).

Buttercup,
My buttercup,

Everywhere rock,
Everywhere snow.

Buttercup,
My buttercup,

Everywhere rock,
Everywhere snow.

Shine on,
Shine on,
Shine on, little sun.

Shine on,
Shine on,
Shine on, little sun.

Your mountain bows.
I bow as well.

Shine on.
Shine on.
Shine on, little sun.

Buttercup,
My buttercup.

In an Oblique Reference to the Pathway between the Living and the Dead, Ernst Dieffenbach Admonishes his Pet Weka.

Weka.
Weka.

In the morning:
chitter,
chatter.

Weka.
Weka.

In the evening:
blither,
blather.

Always busy.
Never lonely.
Always busy.
Never lonely.

Mutter.
Mutter.
Mutter.
Mutter.

Weka.
Weka.

'Mong the living:
chitter,
chatter.

Weka.
Weka.

'Mong the dead:
blither,
blather.

Always busy.
Never lonely.
Always busy.
Never lonely.

Mutter.
Mutter.
Mutter.
Mutter.

In a Haka Celebrating the First European Ascent of that Mountain, Ernst Dieffenbach Compares the Ritual Consumption of his Heart to a Sunset over Taranaki.

Above the flax.
Rise up.
Rise up.

Above the rimu.
Higher.
Higher.

Above the rātā.
Upwards.
Upwards.

To the mountain.
Taranaki.

Cross the river: Mangorake.
Cross the river: Waiwhakaiho.

Tarawainuku: buried deeply.
Arakari: buried deeply.

Who stands there?
Against Pouākai.

Who pines there?
Unloved.
Unloved.

Der Ngeri feiert die Erstbesteigung des Berges Taranaki durch einen Europäer. Ernst Dieffenbach vergleicht den Sonnenuntergang über dem Berg mit dem rituellen Verzehr seines Herzens.

Über dem Flachs.
Steig auf.
Steig auf.

Über dem Rimu.
Höher.
Höher.

Über dem Rātā.
Aufwärts.
Aufwärts.

Zu diesem Berg.
Taranaki.

Quere den Fluss: Mangorake.
Quere den Fluss: Waiwhakaiho.

Tarawainuku: tief vergraben.
Arakari: tief vergraben.

Wer steht hier?
Gegen Pouākai.

Wer schmachtet da?
Ungeliebt.
Ungeliebt.

Who waits there?
Beneath the sun.

Take the ridge.
Tempered. Sharpened.
Take the summit.
Glinting. Striking.
Take the fire.
Burning. Ripening.
At last the fire.
Burning. Ripening.

Here, my tongue.
Take, eat.
Take, eat.

Here, my eyes.
Scoop them.
Scoop them.

Here, my throat.
Gulp it.
Gulp it.

Here, my lungs.
Consume.
Consume.

Red the river: Mangorake.
Red the river: Waiwhakaiho.

Red the rātā.
Flowering. Blooming.
Red the rimu.
Torn asunder.

Wer wartet da?
Unter der Sonne.

Nimm den Grat.
Gehämmert. Angeschärft.

Nimm den Gipfel.
Glitzernd. Prangend.
Nimm das Feuer.
Das Brennen. Auflodern.
Endlich! Das Feuer.
Das Brennen. Auflodern.

Hier, meine Zunge.
Nimm sie, iss.
Nimm sie, iss.

Hier, meine Augen.
Höhle sie aus.
Höhle sie aus.

Hier, meine Kehle.
Schlucke sie.
Schlucke sie.

Hier, meine Lunge.
Verzehre.
Verzehre.

Rot der Fluss: Mangorake.
Rot der Fluss: Waiwhakaiho.

Rot der Rātā.
In Trieben. In Blüte.
Rot der Rimu.
Auseinandergeborsten.

North: the heart.
South: the heart.
East: the heart.
West: the heart.

Take, eat.
Take, eat.
Take, eat.
Take, eat.

North: the heart.
South: the heart.
East: the heart.
West: the heart.

Take, eat.
Take, eat.
Take, eat.
Take, eat.

Nord: das Herz.
Süd: das Herz.
Ost: das Herz.
West: das Herz.

Nimm es, iss.
Nimm es, iss.
Nimm es, iss.
Nimm es, iss.

Nord: das Herz.
Süd: das Herz.
Ost: das Herz.
West: das Herz.

Nimm es, iss.
Nimm es, iss.
Nimm es, iss.
Nimm es, iss.

Following his Early Death from Typhus, Ernst Dieffenbach Considers the Extinction of a Small Bird Carrying His Name in the London Museum of Natural History.

My friend, sometimes it frightens,
I hear the darkness call.
Songs and dreams and fragments,
I fear that this is all.

Your feathers, brown and yellow,
My cloak and shirt of wool,
The daytime and the night-time,
Across each coat must pull.

Can you hear the owl laugh?
The robin in her tree?
I listen for the huia.
Perhaps she'll sing for me.

My friend, sometimes it frightens,
I fear the darkness too.
Songs and dreams and fragments
Are all I have for you.

Songs and dreams and fragments
This one I'll sing for you.

Nach seinem frühen Typhustod bedenkt Ernst Dieffenbach das Aussterben des kleinen Vogels im London Museum of Natural History, der seinen Namen trägt.

Mein Freund, manchmal erschreckt es,
Ruft mich die Finsternis.
Lied und Traum, Fragmente,
Ich fürchte, alles ist's.

Dein Federkleid, braun, gelbe,
Mein Umhang, wollenes Hemd,
Bei Tage und zur Nachtzeit
Ein Rock noch drüber hängt.

Hörst du, wie der Kauz lacht?
Rotkehlchen im Geäst?
Ich lausche auf die Huia,
ob sie sich hören lässt.

Mein Freund, manchmal erschreckt es,
Auch ich fürcht Finsternis.
Lied und Traum, Fragmente
Mehr hab ich nicht für dich.

Lied und Traum, Fragmente,
Dies hier sing ich für dich.

One Hundred and Seventy-Three Years after the Battle of Kāititanga the Descendants of Survivors Treated on the Beach by Ernst Dieffenbach Convey their Gratitude as One Doctor of Te Ati-Awa Pays Respect to Another.

Sawbones, I am singing to say they are well,
those limbs you cracked back into place.
I see them now and then walking past,
a kink here and there, a bow in the shaft.
They are fat with flesh again and noisy.

The wounds have healed of course, been replaced, to heal again.
I recognise your sign, the work was good, have added mine.

That-one-collecting-firewood has a handful of sand
for you off the beach at Kāititanga.
Who knows what it holds? Salt? Shell? Bone?
That memory of your step, perhaps?
It is her gift. It was one of hers you tended that day by the spray.
You belong to her now, in every joint, your thumbprint.

The line of descent is detailed and specific.
It is enough to say, that man you held behind the head,
tipped towards the water, survived,
had a child who had a child
who had a child who one day had her.
She is your mother now, wanders at times,
drifts, back to Kāititanga perhaps.

Perhaps back to you. It is never benign what we do.
Every bandage unravels, ties one line into another.
And so here we have come to each other,
at either end of flesh both of us have loved.

That-one-who-brought-the-thing-together is here as well.
He was present that day, waiting, a foot in both camps, his father
    the enemy of his mother.
Today he prays from the beach, looks out at Kāpiti.
Words curl from his mouth, rise up, look down and thrill
as though set free to become something they would prefer to be.

They weave their way round these I sing to bring you news, keep
    you warm.
Whatever way it works.
There are no boundaries with them.

There are others too. I have held them, listened,
bent their heads towards the water and in them come to you.

Let me be clear. You have loved what I have loved.
In this we are father and son, two ends of a line that stand for now
but in a moment will be drawn in, towards a middle.
There we will be colleagues, brothers.

Past, present, future: what is the fuss?
Go well. Whatever soil holds you now,
you belong to us. This is science too.
How many geographies the heart contains.
For now let us simply take soundings,
hoist the rig and put to sea once more.

Uwe Kolbe

Translations by Glenn Colquhoun

Aëlita

Das war stark, *Dark Sky* in Wellington.
Ich hatte es also vergessen,
das Mädchen der ernsten Träume
für Jahre, vergessen, verloren.
Im Fahrstuhl der Galerie der Wind
auf der Venus, ganz wie vertraut,
da wusste ich wieder Bescheid.
Die Liebe und der Lavafluss,
der Untergang unseres Dieners,
des treuen Roboters,
der einst uns das Leben gerettet.
Frag mich, was Film war, was Leben.

Venus. Ein europäischer Transit mit südlichem Siebengestirn

Vor ihr war Aphrodite, schaumgeboren, nicht römisch, war griechisch, älter als die Griechen, so alt wie der Himmel, ihr Vater, doch seine Tochter, so alt wie das Meer, aber das Meer ist ewig, nicht wahr, aber das Wasser entstand erst, als die Schöpfung voranschritt, als sich die Mutter öffnete, Erde, es freigab, ausdünstete, aber davor, Aphrodites Küche war ein einzig Gemetzel, eitel war sie, wollte die goldene Kugel der Schönsten, bestach einen schlichten Irdischen mit dem Erwerb einer schlichten irdischen Schönheit, ach, und wie viele Helden starben dafür später den Tod, den man später nach ihnen benannte, doch nein, das blutschäumende Metzeln der großen Göttin ist älter, der Knabe auf ihrem Schoß ist ein größerer Gott, Leute, schon als die Erde gebacken wurde, knetete er Blut in sie ein, und, Pankreator, wo warst du, wo war dein Stuhl, als sich die Elemente zum Wasser erfühlten, hattest du Knochen? sage, Christen-Gott, hattest du Knochen? Ja doch, du hast deinen Sohn hergegeben, den Thronfolger, machtest eine Flöte aus Kalk aus ihm, ganz wie das Weiß des Himmels der Neuen Welt, südliche Erde, darüber das Blinzeln der Matariki, die Neugier anderer Göttergeschlechter auf Mensch.

Kafka in Auckland

Aus auf das fremde Licht, Silber des Morgens blass
über der Innenstadt, ging ich die Straße zum Hafen,
fremd wie herein so heraus, das war sicher, stand Kafka
gegenüber, wartete auch auf Grün. Anthrazit seines Anzugs,
hellgraue Krawatte, lang und dünn in der Hose die Beine,
eindeutig orientalisch sanft war, dunkel der Teint.
Als wir aneinander vorübergingen, nahm ich die Streifen
seines Anzuges wahr, elegant war die Kluft, schön
war der Mann, das weiß jeder, der nur ein Foto kennt.
Schon am ersten Tag diesseits des warmen Erdkerns
hatte ich Sehnsucht nach dir, Mitte Europas.

Kafka in Auckland

Drawn into foreign light, the morning
hung silver and pale over the city,
I walked the streets to the port.
Fremd wie herein so heraus, at least this was certain.
Across from me, waiting for a green light, stood Kafka.
His suit was anthracite, his tie light grey,
long and thin in his trousers hung his legs,
his complexion was soft and dark, clearly oriental.
As we passed I noticed the stripes on his suit,
the outfit was elegant, the man was beautiful,
everyone who has seen a photo of him knows that.
Already, this first day on the other side
of the world I longed for you my Europe.

In Transition, Tolaga Bay, 6th June 2012

Ich stand auf der Landungsbrücke / und das vergangene Jahr.
Zahllose Menschen lobten / das Gute, Schöne und Wahre.
Unten warf sich der Geist / an den Beton der Pfeiler.
Spiegelbilder von Wracks / gingen auf große Fahrt.
Eines der schönen Boote der Toten / querte den Horizont.
Der Zeremonienmeister Ngata / blies in das Muschelhorn.
Ich trank aus dem weißen Kelch / das Brechmittel gegen die Lethe.
Die Fürstin kam über das Meer / und fuhr mit ihren feinen Fingern
in meine Augen, die Zeilen entlang, / sie blätterte um mein Gesicht,
die frische, schmerzende Tätowierung, / bis ich ausgelesen war.

Sailor's Time Tunnel

Jahrtausende währende Reise,
ich tauchte und tauchte wie Traum,
es legten sich große Farne herum,
und legten mich an die Leine.
Das hat auf all seinen Fahrten
der Sternenfahrer gut Glück
voraus nicht erhofft, nicht zurück,
mit Ausschauen nicht und mit Rufen
die Jungfrau Erde einmal zu besuchen.

Den Kleiderknüpferinnen vom Te Papa Museum, Wellington, Juni 2012

Nicht eingeweiht zu sein ins Ritual,
dem Beispiel beizuwohnen, Blick, der sagt
ein Hin, ein Her, die Freundlichkeit der Fremden,
die voreinander Bilder überblenden.

Wir kennen das und fragen nicht zuviel
und machen draus das gute, leichte Spiel.
Kalanikupules, des Königs, Mantel,
einst Cook geschenkt, zum Artefakt gewandelt,

wir spürten noch die Macht als Licht von innen,
bevor wir zu den Knüpferinnen gingen,
die heute unvermindert leicht den Bast
auf ihren Schenkeln spleißen, und es fast

vergessen lassen, dass wir vor uns sehen,
wie wir schon selbst eingehen in Museen.

To the clothing-weavers, Te Papa Museum, Wellington, June 2012

Not formally privy to secrets,
examples regardless still teach us:
'Look now, be friendly to strangers',
weaves place into face into faces.

We nod and don't ask any questions,
a game played politely, invented,
Kalanikupule's cloak meantime, a dream,
once gifted to Cook waits, a thing.

Its power holds still, the light dappled,
and within it the weavers entangle
who now rub their thighs with the bast,
who now rub their thighs with the past,

almost lost, what we see in each seam,
how we too are stitched into museums.

Aus einem arroganten Land

Aus einem arroganten Land komme ich,
da weiß ich die Namen, habe sie selbst
im Überschwang reichlich verteilt,
ob eines es wollte, ob nicht, an Hahn
und an Henne, an Busch, Baum und Blüte,
sie tragen die Namen wie angeklebt.
Das Land ist hintern Horizont gesunken,
in Weltmeer, in Luftmeer, in Flut,
höher als das gewohnte Entkommen,
das Ausmaß an Sünde ist endlich so.
Nun zieht die Sonne namenlos droben
und spurlos die Frau ohne Mund vorbei.

I come from an arrogant country

I come from an arrogant country.
I know of names, have myself,
in exuberance, freely given them out,
whether they were wanted or not: to the rooster
and the hen, to the bush, the bark, the blossom.
They bear their names as if glued on.

But now this land has sunk beneath the horizon,
in sky-sea, in sea-sky,
a tide higher than usual required.
Such, finally, is the magnitude of sins.
Here the sun moves namelessly
and the mouthless woman passes by without sound.

Keine

Es gab keine Vorwarnung, leider.
Ich hatte wie üblich Probleme,
stand fremd in der Landschaft
und hoffte, die Fürstin verstieße
mich nicht, elend war's, alles klar.
In solchen Fällen schaute ich immer
zum Himmel auf, wusste, wohin.
Nur diesmal ging nichts, die Sterne,
in Konstellationen auch hier,
sie waren mir unbekannt
und halfen nicht.

Tupaia

Er strich den Bart auf Unendlich, Viermal und Sieben. Wind heulte, und Wolken verbargen den Stern mit der Idee eines höheren Wesens. Er tilgte alle Zahlen vom Papier und faltete den Zugvogel daraus. Über dem Tisch der Palmzweig, das Bett in der Form eines Boots. Seine Liebe lag da, noch fern der Sehnsucht der Franzosen. Schamanenblut schäumte selten, er nahm ihr kräftiges Kinn, sie streckte die Zunge heraus und sagte das Zauberwort auf unanständige Weise. Nach der Erfindung der Liebe kam Land in Sicht, kamen Schüsse, Entführung, Probleme beim Übersetzen. Schade, Tupaia.

Whakapapa 2012

Nicht aufschreiben, aber weitersagen.
Abtasten den Strand mit dem bloßen Fuß.
Wie blind auf dem Neuland, nicht wie damals
Cook und seine Leute, vor 243 Jahren,
nicht so, mit Waffen in Händen, Kommandos.
Weitersagen unter dem Druck des Winds,
schnellem Gleiten der Boote der Toten.
Noch ist er heiß, der Glutkern der Erde,
dir unter den Füßen, heiß sind die Wasser
tief in den Wäldern Morere, kein Zweifel,
das ist eine Insel, eben geborenes Land,
sie wird sich weiter erheben, wir werden
anders erscheinen, aber das schreib nicht,
bist kein Prophet, nimm nur, was jetzt ist,
das Gleiten der Boote der Toten, träumend
am Pier von Uawa, Tolaga Bay, geneigt
zum Gesang und dem Stampfen der Füße
derer, die da sind, von alters so jung.
Nicht aufschreiben, aber weitersagen.

Brigitte Oleschinski
Paki,* half-cooked

Neuseeländische Notizen (Auszüge)
New Zealand notes (excerpts)

Translations by Chris Price

Dauernd bin ich Gerüchten

auf der Spur, oder mein Gedächtnis hält für Gerüchte, was ich doch
schon erlebt habe, anwesend, oder wenigstens nachgeschlagen,
dauernd aber verschwindet das Erlebte, das Gewußte, als wäre es
mir entgangen. Einem Gerücht nach das Kreuz des Südens gesehen;
in welcher sternklaren Nacht denn. Blaugrün. Grünblau. Eine
Venus mit grünen Lippen. Was sie sagte: Die Tinte sei schwarz,
mit der ihnen die Moko gestochen werden, besser: geritzt. Aber
in der Māori-DNA gebe es ein Enzym, das die Hautzeichen später
grün färbt. Grünblau. Blaugrün. Dann tiefblaues Wasser am
Küstensaum entlang, von oben sehen die sanft gefalteten Hänge
der Hügel hellgrün aus, eher smaragdfarben, wir fliegen in einem
zwölfsitzigen Kanu.

I'm always in pursuit

of rumours, or I recall as rumour what I've actually experienced here, or at least looked up, but what's known and done is always vanishing, as if it slipped my mind. There's a rumour that I've seen the Southern Cross; but on which clear-starred night was that? Bluegreen. Greenblue. A green-lipped Venus. What she said was: black ink is used to etch the moko. In Māori DNA, though, there's an enzyme that will turn skin-symbols green. Greenblue. Bluegreen. Then water deep-blue along coastal seams, from high above the gently folding slopes of hills are brilliant emerald green, we're flying in a twelve-seater canoe.

Auch die Kleider

fliegen, sie bellen ein bißchen von innen und wehen, flattern, segeln. Lange seien die beiden Inseln ohne Säugetiere geblieben, nur ein paar Fledermäuse verschlug es in diese einsame Gegend. Alles hatte Federn oder Schuppen, oder Panzer, Schalen, Gehäuse. Dann legten die Kanus an, Hunde und Ratten gingen mit an Land. Tierseelen. Baumseelen. Fremde Götterfamilien richteten sich ein. Mit ihnen vermehrten sich Abkömmlinge, Namen und Gesänge, Dingseelen. Den einheimischen Vögeln bekamen die Menschen nicht. Oft bekamen auch die Menschen den Menschen nicht. Aber nun hinaus ins Weiße des Weltraums!, sagt mein Alien. Zur Ablenkung, denn eben stieß ich mit den Zehen an eine Handvoll toter Federn, ein wie schlafender Sperling, über den eine Straße Ameisen zieht. Schon stolpern wir in der Tolaga-Bucht übereinander, Silben und Setzlinge, blind hinter schwarzen Brillen. Auch die Brillen bellen, innen.

Even the clothes

are flying, and they bark a little, inwardly, they wave and flutter, sail. For a long time these two islands had no mammals other than a few bats that had fetched up in this forsaken place. Everything was feathered or scaled, armoured, shelled, encased. Then the canoes came ashore, and the rats and dogs came with them. Animal souls. The souls of trees. Whole families of foreign gods settled in. And their scions multiplied, names and songs, the souls of things. The native birds just couldn't cope with people. Often the people couldn't cope with people. But now, out into the whiteness of the cosmos! says my Alien. As a distraction, since at that very moment my toe had stubbed a fistful of dead feathers, a sparrow as if sleeping, marched over by a regiment of ants. In Tolaga Bay we were already tripping over one another, syllables and seedlings, blind behind dark glasses. The glasses, too, were barking, inwardly.

Nur das Weiße des Weltraums

über uns, draußen und drinnen, wintertags früh sehe ich,
vielleicht, den Morgenstern über den Glasrippen, unter denen
das dunkle Poolwasser schwappt. Der Pool klebt auf halber Höhe
an der Hotelwand wie ein Hängebauchschwein. Sehr warmes
Wasser unter Riesenfarnen und Cabbage trees, rundum rauscht
der Regen, das Kiwi-Englisch rauscht im Ohr. Nur dass Alien, als
wäre er taub heute, nicht mit mir spricht. Oder ich höre ihn nicht.
Ein anderes Gerücht war noch gar nicht fertig; die Künstlerin
ließ mich anschauen, was sie eben auspackte: Roben, Kostüme.
Nachgeschneidert den frühen Entdeckern und Siedlern, gekreuzt
mit Māori-Stoffen und Māori-Mustern. Federfarben. Flachsfarben.
Rote Blüten, eingestickt, an ihren Bäumen sah ich sie zittern wie
kleine Pelztiere. Dann läuft über den Boden ein eingelegtes Band
aus Pāua-Muscheln, es trennt Zeitschichten und Info-Tafeln. Ein
Tafelmesser, ein Papiermesser und eine Muschelklinge kämmen im
Halbkreis Flachssträhnen aus. Die Spur der Zaubersprüche verliert
sich im Video-Gemurmel. Alien, flüstere ich. Keine Antwort.

Only the whiteness of the cosmos

above us, inside and out, on this early winter's day maybe I'm seeing the morning star above the pool's dark water lapping under glass rafters. Halfway up the hotel wall, the pool protrudes like a potbellied pig. Hot springs under giant ferns and cabbage trees, the rain hisses round me like the white noise of Kiwi English in my ears. Only my Alien, as though mute today, won't talk to me. Or I can't hear him. Another rumour was still incomplete; the artist let me see what she'd just unpacked: gowns and costumes. Tailored early-settler style, mixed with Māori materials and motifs. Feather-coloured. Flax-coloured. Embroidered with red blossoms I'd seen trembling like small furred creatures on the trees. A strip of pāua inlay running across the floor, dividing time layers and interpretation panels. A table-knife, a paper-knife and a mussel-blade comb out the flax strands in a semi-circle. The spells' echo gets lost in video-murmur. Alien, I whisper. No answer.

Wenigstens wiegt er

nichts, nicht im Frachtbauch, nicht im Handgepäck, er flog unter oder über uns, die ganzen zwanzigtausend Kilometer in einem einzigen Gedanken. Innen aber wir, langgestreckter Silberleib, der die Datumsgrenzen überquert, silbenheckender Langstreckenleib, und bewegte sich auf die lange weiße Wolke zu, Aotearoa, aber das dachte ich noch nicht, ich dachte nur, mit meiner Kinderstimme, -seeland . . . , -seeland . . . – Die Plejaden nicht gesehen, wide asleep, mit denen hier das Jahr beginnt. Dafür im Aufzug das Geräusch der Venuswinde. Damit fuhr ich hinauf in die Eingangsschleuse, eine durchsichtige Sphäre aus Galaxienhaut. Wie lange sie daran gerechnet haben. Allein der Kulturenverbrauch, und immer neue Ursuppenwürfel. Die Venuswinde tragen mich weiter als jedes andere Gerücht. Am Rand ein Präriegras, das seinen Namen zwitschert, hinter dem lange zergangenen Termitenhügel. Die blaugrüne Küstenlinie, kaum einen Lichtsekundenbruchteil alt. Und in Parsec noch ein bisschen jünger.

At least he weighs

nothing, not in the cargo hold, not in my carry-on, he must have
flown above us, or below, the whole twenty-thousand kilometres
in the blink of an idea. But we were in that elongated silver body
crossing datelines, in that long-distance body spinning syllables,
travelling towards the long white cloud, Aotearoa, but I wasn't
thinking that yet, I was only thinking, in my child's voice, -sealand
. . . , sealand . . . –Wide asleep, I missed the Pleiades, which usher
in the New Year here. Instead, I heard the winds of Venus in the
lift. In it, I ascended to the airlock, a transparent sphere made with
the skin of galaxies. How long did it take them to come up with
that? The sheer number of cultures they'd have gone through, and
the endless new cubes of ur-soup. The winds of Venus have carried
me further than any other rumour. At the outer limit, prairie grass
is chirruping its name beside a long-demolished termite hill. The
bluegreen coastline barely a fraction of a light-second old. And in
Parsecs younger still.

Den ersten Planeten

schon ruiniert! höre ich mich draußen sagen, ein blasser
Melatoninwert unter dem weißen, weißen Licht. Falls es der erste
Planet war. An der Rezeption arbeitet wieder der lange schwarze
Mantel; es wird nicht geheizt. Wir sehen einen geschnitzten Mann
mit Kopf und Hals in einer Vulva verschwinden. My mum rolled
two beer bottles together for a pillow, erzählt uns der Artefakt-
Experte. Wenn kein passender Stein zu finden war als Kissen.
Vulva. Venus. Nein, auch die glutrote Sonnenscheibe nicht mit
eigenen Augen gesehen. Die eine, wandernde Pupille. Schwört eine
Brille in Berlin, dass doch. Fataler Versuch des Geschnitzten, der
Totengöttin die Unsterblichkeit zu stehlen. Das weiß der Mythen-
Experte. Māui, der einst Aotearoa aus der See fischte und die Sonne
einfing. Aber weiter gehen wir nicht!, schlimmstenfalls dieses eine
Sonnensystem. Schwör mir, Alien, weiter nicht.

The first planet

ruined already! I hear myself declare outside, pale melatonin under
the white, white light. If it *was* the first planet. A long black coat
is working on the reception desk again; there's no heating. We
see a carved man whose head and neck are disappearing inside a
vulva. My mum rolled two beer bottles together for a pillow, said
the artefact curator. If there wasn't a suitable stone. Vulva. Venus.
No, I didn't even see the sun's glowing red-gold retina with my
own eyes. Nor its single, wandering pupil either. But *I* did, swears
a pair of glasses in Berlin. The carved one's fatal attempt to wrest
eternal life from the goddess of death. The myth-curator knows
the story: Māui, who fished up Aotearoa from the sea and caught
the sun. But we must go no further than one solar system, tops.
Promise me, Alien, no further.

Venustransit, kopfunter 1 – Antipodenwitze

Wie schön leucht' uns der Morgenstern.
—Philipp Nicolai, 1597

Das kann man ähnlich auch auf Māori sagen: Mehemea ko Kōpū e rere ana i te pae.

Zwar gibt es in der Überlieferung der Māori auch andere Namen für die Venus. Als Abendstern kann sie anders heißen als im Sommer, doch ihr häufigster Name scheint Kōpū zu sein. Sternbilder waren wichtig für die seefahrenden polynesischen Stämme, die Neuseeland zwischen dem 11. und 13. Jahrhundert besiedelten. Gut fünfhundert Jahre also vor den europäischen Siedlern, denen James Cook im Auftrag der britischen Krone die Doppelinsel zugänglich machte.

„Anstrengend, eh?", fragt der Busfahrer. Unbewegten Gesichts, nur die Augen glitzern.

Ja, wir sind wieder im blauen Bus, wir steigen zum dritten oder vierten Mal wieder ein. Vorn an der Scheibe klebt das Logo Transit-Of-Venus in der richtigen Farbe. Inzwischen kennt der Busfahrer die Delegierten, die in seinen Bus gehören. Höchstens die Hälfte sind Kiwis, echte Neuseeländer. Dafür fast alle Wissenschaftler. Viele Tweedjacken, wenige Frauen. Dazu die bunten Vögel aus Europa: Poets from Germany.

„Immer so mit dem Kopf nach unten hängen, eh?" Jetzt geht das Glitzern langsam in ein Grinsen über.

Ich stutze noch, in meinem langsameren Englisch, dann muss ich mitlachen. Der Antipodenwitz funktioniert in beide Richtungen. Dabei sind wir, nach sechsunddreißig Stunden Flug, tatsächlich down under und upside down, im Jetlag und wide asleep. Kommen aus dem Sommer in den Winter, der hier, im oberen Drittel der Nordinsel, noch halbwegs warm ist. Auf der Südinsel schneit es schon.

Northness ... , höre ich später in einem neuseeländischen Gedicht, bedeutet den Einheimischen die feuchtwarmen Träume

von pazifischem Türkis. Werden südliche Winde angekündigt, greift alles nach Schals, Handschuhen und Mützen.

Die zeitgenössische deutsche Lyrik reist in vielen Facetten. Fast jede Autorin, jeder Autor scheint überall schon einmal gewesen zu sein, zumindest weitläufig in der Nähe. Australien? Klar. Bis Singapur kenne ich im Schlaf. Meist geht es um internationale Poesie-Festivals, Auftritte, Lesungen, die Zusammenarbeit mit anderen Künsten, Bühnen, Medien.

Aber noch nie in Neuseeland!, sagten wir, unisono, bei der Ankunft.

Neuseeland ist uns neu. Wir haben ein paar hastig zusammengelesene Wikipedia-Artikel im Kopf, aber lieber nicht zuviel davon. Über die Sitzlehnen hinweg, im dämmrigen Flieger, hatten wir angelegentlich über das Projekt spekuliert. Doch eigentlich ist alles offen.

Venustransit. Versschmuggel.

Schon die drei deutschen Poets könnten unterschiedlicher kaum sein. Dasselbe gilt für die drei neuseeländischen Gegenüber.

Als wir am Vorabend des Venustransits in Gisborne aufeinandertreffen, verschmelzen hinter unserem Rücken die Presse-, Logistik-, Koordinationsteams von einem halben Dutzend Veranstaltern. Was sie monatelang geplant haben, sollen wir nun in echte Erlebnisse verwandeln.

Und danach in Berlin in noch echtere Gedichte.

Venustransit, kopfunter 2 – Tolaga Bay am Tag des Venustransits

Der Nasengruß fällt leider aus.

Als wir morgens zu den Delegierten der Transit-Of-Venus-Konferenz in die langen Busse steigen, bilden wir eine stolze Kolonne von gut zweihundert Teilnehmern, die in vier Bussen Richtung Tolaga Bay befördert werden. Oder Uawa, wie die Gegend auf Māori heißt. Es ist der Strand, an dem James Cook auf seiner Weltumseglung 1769 in Neuseeland schließlich an Land ging.

Wer das noch nicht wußte, lernt es auf der Fahrt. Lizzy vom

Stamm Te Aitanga-a-Hauiti ist für jede Ignoranz gerüstet. Sie veranstaltet mit uns ein Quiz.

„Wie nennen wir Neuseeland auf Māori?" – Aotearoa, rufen wir im Chor.

„Who knows what that means?" – Lange weiße Wolke, rufen wir. Klatschen, kleine Belohnungen. Wer kommt von ganz weit weg? – The Germans, werden wir verpfiffen. Müssen wir jetzt was singen?

Wir in den Bussen kommen aus der halben Welt und beiden Inseln Neuseelands, aber Tausende mehr strömen am frühen Morgen aus der nächsten Umgebung zusammen. Tolaga Bay ist das angestammte Land von Māori-Gemeinden, die nicht von weißen Siedlern um ihren Grund und Boden gebracht wurden.

Aussteigen zum traditionellem Empfang in einem reichverzierten Marae, dem zeremoniellen Gemeindehaus. Wir sind Neulinge hier und eindeutig Pākehā, aber im Halbschlaf. Die Unter- und Obertöne des Tages träume ich für später mit. Jetzt folge ich blind Hinemoana Baker über eine sumpfige Wiese. Die Frauen zuerst. Wir werden durch das geschnitzte Tor geleitet und unter Zeltplanen nach rechts, auf die Gästeseite. Hinter den gedrängten Rücken der anderen höre ich der furchterregenden Darbietung eines Haka zu. Jaaah, traditioneller Begrüßungstanz.

Hätte ich doch die vorab gemailten Instruktionen gelesen. Hätte ich im Netz nach den einschlägigen Clips gefischt. Ich hätte hier dasselbe gehört, aber halb so verblüfft. Brüllende Kriegerstimmen, vielerlei Stampfen und Prusten, dazwischen die Frauenstimmen, die von melodischem Gesang unvermittelt in Schreien wechseln.

Anderntags sehe ich auch die Bilder. Erkenne die Jugendlichen des Uawa-Gebiets in ihren grünen Transit-of-Venus-Shirts. Den ganzen Tag lang sind sie den Besuchergruppen zugeteilt als witzige, fröhliche Babysitter. Im Haka aber dominieren die bedrohlichen Gebärden, das Augenrollen und Zungerausstrecken, das Fuchteln und Um-sich-Schlagen.

Ein Ritual, das die Fremden auf Nervenstärke und Respekt prüft.

Kurz stelle ich mir die Jugendlichen zuhause in Neukölln vor, im Wettstreit der diversen Straßen-Identitäten. Die Gestik der

Māori wirkt mühelos überlegen.

Once were warriors . . . –

Dann der abrupte Übergang in schwelgerische Gastfreundschaft: Kaffee, Imbiss. Hier fehlt nun das eigentliche Bindeglied. Nur ein paar hastige Repräsentanten haben Zeit für den Hongi, sprich: den Nasengruß. Aber der Terminplan drängt.

Dabei haben wir mit Hinemoana Baker geübt. Seltsamste Intimität, wie sich Stirn an Stirn, Nasenrücken an Nasenrücken legt und man gemeinsam – nun ja, schnauft.

Venustransit, kopfunter 3 – Eine sehr dunkle Orange

Diesmal entlässt uns der Bus in das festliche Gedränge direkt an der Tolaga-Bucht. Hier führt die längste Pier der südlichen Hemisphäre angemessen weit hinaus ins Wasser, die Mündung des Flusses Uawa schneidet links und rechts hohe Felsen entzwei, der Strand legt sich als sachte Biegung unter den wolkenverhangenen Himmel. Mehr Programm aus Reden und Führungen, Schulkinder spielen die Landung von James Cook nach – aus der Māori-Perspektive –, es wird Essen aus dem Erdofen geben und eine Wiederaufforstungsaktion, bei der wir alle ein Bäumchen setzen am anderen Ende der Welt. Aber die Blicke gehen doch besorgt in die Wolken. Wenn die Sonne unsichtbar bleibt, werden wir auch den wandernden Punkt nicht sehen.

Wo suche ich überhaupt? Linksverkehr und linksdrehende Türknöpfe, selbst die Riegelchen der Klotüren schnappen falschherum ein. Empire-Echos. Dreht sich auch die Sonne anders? Nimmt der Mond andersrum zu oder ab?

In Berlin ist es jetzt kurz nach Mitternacht, hier schon zehn Uhr morgens. Viele der Kinder tragen Schuluniformen mit Māori-Aufschriften, blaue Jacken, weiße Hemden, dazu die eckigen schwarzen Pappbrillen, die einen beim Aufsetzen auf der Stelle in tiefstes Dunkel tauchen. Während die Reden beginnen – Dual Heritage, Shared Future –, werden die Wolken ein bisschen dünner.

Und noch dünner.

Aus Berlin bekomme ich später ein Foto zugeschickt, das dort

gegen fünf Uhr morgens aufgenommen worden ist, gleich nach
Sonnenaufgang auf dem Teufelsberg. Inzwischen haben wir in der
Tolaga-Bucht drei Uhr nachmittags, der schwarze Punkt ist in den
Teleskopbildern am unteren Rand der Sonnenscheibe von links
nach rechts gewandert. Auf dem Foto aus Berlin wandert er von
rechts nach links. Und natürlich oben entlang.

Was ich wirklich gesehen habe? Nicht auf einem Bildschirm,
nicht im Teleskop?

Die Sonne hinter der Brille war eine sehr dunkle Orange.

Der Punkt ein Gerücht.

Dauernd war ich Gerüchten auf der Spur –

Brigitte Oleschinski and Chris Price
[Dear Venus]

An anachronous *cadavre exquis* poem on postcards
to/from Wellington and Berlin, 2012

Ein aus der Zeit gefallenes *Cadavre exquis*-Gedicht auf Postkarten
von/nach Wellington, 2012

[Dear Venus]

If you are a black dot on a white disk
I am a black dish on a white cloth

> *that wipes the lens with a streak of light*
> *no natural eye could envisage –*

except when these moonswung lovers, shoes just
inches off the ground, look up from their lives

> *with the mildly cock-eyed gaze of*
> *Venus, and from a thousand*
> *crater-eyes the moon stares back:*

observatory of dust, it draws
a star-crossed orbit round them

> *studied by alien sight-organs*
> *that can't identify them in the crooked dark*

through the rain of stars that hurry
past the windscreen of the spacecraft

> *and Venus swings back, like a windscreen wiper*
> *against the patter of black particles, white waves*

like a golf club thwacking the pockmarked moon
once more round her earthly course

like a pool cue sinking the white ball
in a lover's black pocket.

[Dear Venus]

Bist du ein schwarzer Punkt auf einer weißen Scheibe
bin ich ein weißer Teller auf einem schwarzen Tisch

> *wischt sich im Strich*
> > *durch die Linse, Licht*
> *wie kein natürliches Auge es ermisst –*

außer, diese mondgewiegten Liebenden mit den Schuhen
halbhoch in der Luft, blickten auf aus ihrem Leben

> *so sanfter Silberblick der Venus-*
> > *pupille, aus tausend Krateraugen*
> *starrt der Mond zurück –*

Sternwarte aus Staub, die sie einhüllt
in eine Umlaufbahn aus Sternenstäuben

> *observiert von fremden Sehorganen, keins*
> > *das uns kennt in seiner dunklen*
> > *Krümmung –*

unter Sternenregen, der über
die Windschutzscheibe ihres Raumgleiters gischtet

> *und schwingt zurück, die Venusschaukel*
> > *wie ein Scheibenwischer gegen das Prasseln*
> *von schwarzen Teilchen, weißen Wellen –*

wie ein Golfschläger, der den pockennarbigen Mond
frisch in die Erdumlaufbahn drischt

wie ein Billardstock, der die weiße Kugel
im schwarzen Liebessack versenkt.

Chris Price

Translations by Brigitte Oleschinski

Fort Venus

We chase the goddess
round the planet till she falls
exhausted in her seven sisters'
arms. How far we pry, in our
makeshift island hides.
We wholly disrespect
the privacies of sky. When

she comes, draped in romantic
mists, with a diadem of feathers
green and red that scatters
and refracts, we're ready:
we brandish pen and ink
at first, and then unholster
photographic revolvers.
To the naked she's fully clad
but our spyglass strips her.
From some she shyly turns

her face, but we are unperturbed –
the spurned set off in search
of other lovers while we take
her measurements with
astronomical clocks and
quadrants. We picture her from
every angle, elevation: a distant
kind of love, or its relation.

In pursuance of His Majesty's
Pleasure we do not take
sides. We try to listen to
the local guides, even if
their tongues are thick with

Fort Venus

Wir jagen die Göttin
rund um den ganzen Planeten, bis sie
erschöpft in die Arme ihrer Sieben
Schwestern fällt. Wie tief wir in sie dringen
aus unseren windschiefen Inselverstecken.
Wir scheren uns keinen Deut um die
Privatsphäre des Himmels. – Wenn

sie erscheint, in romantische Nebel
gehüllt, in einem Diadem aus Federn,
die grün und rot zerstieben
und splittern, sind wir bereit:
Erst schwingen wir die Federhalter,
dann entsichern wir
die Fotorevolver.
Den Nackten scheint sie verhüllt,
doch unsere Fernrohre ziehen sie aus.
Von manchen wendet scheu

sie das Gesicht, doch wir bleiben ungerührt –
die Verschmähten suchen sich andere
Geliebte, während wir ihre Maße nehmen
mit astronomischen Uhren und
Viertelkreismessern. Wir fixieren sie

aus jedem Winkel, jedem Aufriss: eine Liebe
aus der Ferne, ein Verhältnis fast.

Im Verfolg der Wünsche Seiner
Majestät schlagen wir uns auf keine
Seite. Wir hören den einheimischen
Informanten zu, obwohl ihre Zungen
überwuchert sind von fremden

unfamiliar jungles. We eat
their greens, record the species,
pick up a few crude words,
some temporary brides, and plant
gunpowder, children and
V.D. The goddess won't

be back this way for a century
or so, but just now she is at home
on every isle. We seize the day.

Dschungeln. Wir essen
ihr Grünzeug, verzeichnen die Art,
legen uns ein paar rohe Wörter zu,
Bräute auf Zeit, und säen
Schießpulver aus, Kinder und
Geschlechtskrankheiten. Die Göttin

kommt hier ein Jahrhundert oder so
nicht mehr vorbei, aber jetzt gerade ist sie
auf jeder Insel daheim. Wir ergreifen
die Gelegenheit.

Poedua

If you are a black dot on a white disk
    I am a black dish on a white cloth.

If you are a bright spot in my dark sky
    I am a wide dish receiving white noise.

If I am elliptical, capricious,
    you are point-to-pinpoint accurate.

If you are a white-draped goddess
    I am your ear's black pearl.

If you are a singular sceptre
    I am a quarrel of feathered chiefs.

If I am a Polynesian princess
    you are the red Queen and

when you speak, I lose my voice and
    when I stand mute before you

on a painted wall, you see stars –
    my innumerable motu

dazzle your rocky shores.
    Now your world is no more

than a cloudy blue bead
    at my throat but I foresee

the day it inundates me in
    the way you repaint

Poedua

Bist du ein schwarzer Punkt auf einer weißen Scheibe,
  bin ich ein schwarzer Teller auf einem weißen Tisch.

Bist du ein heller Fleck an meinem dunklen Himmel,
  bin ich eine weite Schüssel für das weiße Rauschen.

Bin ich elliptisch, unberechenbar,
  bist du auf den Punkt punktgenau.

Bist du eine weiß-drapierte Göttin,
  bin ich dein schwarzer Perlohrring.

Bist du ein einziges Zepter,
  bin ich ein Gequengel von Häuptlingsfedern.

Bin ich die polynesische Prinzessin,
  bist du die rote Königin und

wenn du sprichst, verliere ich die Stimme, und
  wenn ich stumm vor dir stehe

auf einer Leinwand, siehst du Sterne –
  meine unzähligen Inseln

blenden deine felsgrauen Küsten.
  Deine Welt ist nun nichts

als eine milchig blaue Perle
  an meiner Kehle, aber ich ahne

den Tag, an dem sie mich überflutet,
  so wie du mein Gesicht

my face. If you are hungry
    I will feed you, but

I'm not so sure that you'll
    return the courtesy.

übermalst. Bist du hungrig,
    will ich dich füttern, doch

bin ich nicht sicher, dass du
    die Höflichkeit erwiderst.

Parallax

While you were sleeping
we went looking for the circle
of least confusion. We could not look

direct for fear of blindness
but took a Gregorian telescope
to reverse the view.

*

As we stepped warily into
the circle of least confusion,
the black drop

foxed us, making readings
imprecise. Had it travelled
with us as a speck

on the lens?
We resolved
to try again.

*

Our hands moved forward
saying *nails* and *cloth*.
Theirs replied with
crayfish, water.

We touched hands in
the circle of least confusion
thinking ourselves brothers.

When we said *trade*
they said *exchange*. We thought
they meant the same.

*

Drawing our location
was a way to take it
in, to take it home,

a way to make it in
our language which was
all we had for

a drawstring to close
the circle of least
confusion.

*

While you were sleeping
we were dreaming awake.
What we thought we knew

of the sunlit world
travelled astronomical
units back to you

squaring the circle
of least confusion.
There is of course

another version.

It is good to speak the language of New Zealand

What dost thou want here?
I am very hungry.
Go thou. Sit thou.
Tomorrow return.

Wilt thou drink water?
I am very thirsty.
Fetch some sea water.
Yes! I will drink.

Where art thou going?
Fetch some good water.
I am well. I am ill.
The sun is set.

Where art thou going?
I love thee. I hate thee.
I go to Tippoona.
Tomorrow return.

What dost thou want here?
How many? How many?
I am ill. I am well.
Let us sit down and eat.

Kapi ta karakea a koraro no New Zealand

Aána a koe ekona?
Kamátte aou e te eaki.
Ire attoo ra. Ekoua ra.
Apopo ka yooke mi.

Kaenu a koea ta whi?
Kamátte aou e ta whi.
Tara ta whi moana.
Ai! kaenu aoa.

Kohaa a koea ka ire?
Tara ta whi maoude.
Koou ta oura. Koou ta mátte.
Kapo tu ra.

Kohaa a koea ka ire?
Karaoha aou ke eakoe. Kakeno aou ke eakoe.
Aire éna ou ke Tippoona.
Appopo ka yooke mi.

Aána a koe ekona?
Toko hea? Toko hea?
Koou ta mátte. Koou ta oura.
Irenui taooa kekone kiei.

The audition

I auditioned for a band called the High Rising Terminals but
I wasn't born in this country.

Are you mono, bi or multi-culti?
English will do for most

people, but the tūī considers it a crude
approximation of his native foliage.

I sleep on my right-hand side here – one cheek
rests on water

one sea-ear listens for round vowels rising from
the mussel's razor lips.

There is much I could have told you but I no longer
have it by heart.

Do you too hear the rain that raineth every day
as you lie on your bed of nails?

Have you armed the clattering cabbage-tree?
Can you translate for me

this basket of steam, that slow pulsing
underneath the ground?

Das Vorsprechen

Ich sprach vor bei einer Band namens Signalphonetiker, aber dafür
bin ich im falschen Land geboren.

Bist du mono, bi oder multi-kulti?
Den meisten Leuten reicht

Englisch, aber der Tūī hält das nur für eine grobe
Näherung an sein heimisches Blattwerk.

Ich schlafe hier auf meiner rechten Seite – eine Wange
ruht auf Wasser,

ein Seeohr horcht auf die runden Vokale, die
aufsteigen aus den Rasiermesserlippen einer Muschel.

Ich wollte dir noch viel mehr erzählen, doch
es ist mir entfallen.

Hörst du den Regen regnen alle Tage,
wenn du schmachtest auf deinem Nagelbett?

Hast du den klirrenden Lanzenbaum bewaffnet?
Übersetzt du mir diesen dampfenden

Bastkorb, den langsamen Puls
tief in der Erde?

Venera

Fictions at an exhibition, Adam Art Gallery, Wellington, June 2012

You might choose the bigger picture:
Venus erasing Matariki
with her heavenly contrail.
Or pick the photo where a single
fictitious star perturbs
the empirical firmament.
After all, you're more inclined
to put on history's weight.

In the political sky, satellite spies.
In the polluted sky, space junk.

Down home, though, we've been busy
twirling our torches like poi
on the front lawn, while indoors,
in a darkened room, happy couples
are swigging beer and swinging
on the moon. By the front porch,
our starry night has painted
a black window, and in the lift's

three-storey space capsule, we're
taking turns at playing Māui
re-entering the muffled soundscape
of his goddess-mother's womb before
she crushes his headstrong fantasy flat
as an aluminium can. No worries though –
you're weightless here. Just press

the silver button to release
the seal and you're back
in the gallery where
the black rubber floors
suit our black rubber souls.
Come on, let's push the inflatable out
on the night's wide waters, see
how far it goes.

Antipodean

I am the wrong
way round, my north,
your south, my up,
your down, your Krone
my Crown. My dark side,
your light, my loose,
your tight, your arse
my face, your paradise
my place. My trees
line your sleep. Your sleep
leaves my trees. I sail a
counter-clockwise water,
your moon's a
measurable daughter.
It's your gift, my loan.
Your terror cove, my home.
Your page, my mouth.
My north, your south.

Transit of Venus: A reVERSible Project

An interview with Uwe Kolbe,
Brigitte Oleschinski and Ulrike Almut Sandig
by Aurélie Maurin

Interview with Uwe Kolbe, Brigitte Oleschinski and Ulrike Almut Sandig

You travelled south to observe the transit like the crew of the Endeavour in 1769. Can we see you as Captain Cook's 'descenders'?

Uwe: Now that you put it that way, I'd say the description fits us perfectly. We really were Cook's descenders, or descenders after Cook. Granted, we didn't spend months at sea, we arrived by plane with no recorded casualties, and our skill set was rather less diverse. But then we stood under the white light of the southern skies and looked down at the waves of the Pacific where Cook anchored the *Endeavour* in 1769. Like him, we encountered Māori from different tribes – among them faces I knew only from Gauguin. We saw tattooed men and watched incredibly physical rituals that would have been terrifying if it hadn't been for the eruptions of merriment. It brought to life the misunderstandings that apparently arose between Cook and the local Māori. Cook was lucky enough to have a guide: the great shaman Tupaia from Tahiti, who served as an interpreter and mediator. Tahiti was where the party observed and recorded the transit of Venus, which was the purpose of Cook's voyage.

But for all the historical associations, what really struck me about our visit to Gisborne and Tolaga Bay wasn't the parallels between the two journeys. Whatever their heritage, contemporary New Zealanders share a profound sense of responsibility for their country, its landscape and unique natural features. You can see and feel their identification with the land everywhere you go. Foreigners aren't made to feel foreign in a place where new residents are accorded proper rights from the outset, and where people have learned to live alongside each other since Cook's time. I'd like to see that imported to my country.

Ulrike: Very few of my thoughts were devoted to Cook. I imagine the transit of Venus looked much the same to him as it did to us.

He probably saw a very distant sun, too small for him to make out Venus. Then he will have looked through a telescope and at last seen the beauty of the minuscule black dot – exactly as I saw it. It's an odd thing to witness an event that must have looked identical when it last took place on a specific historical date. The next transit of Venus will be on 11 September 2117 and none of the people we know and love will have the slightest chance of seeing it. Now that's even harder to process.

Brigitte: I wasn't expecting anything to be especially foreign because so much of New Zealand seems to have come from Europe or North America and been relocated more expansively amid spectacular natural scenery and sheep. Lots of things surprised me, but three stand out. First, the most striking upside-down oddity is that the cold always comes from the south. You can rationalise it beforehand, but then it hits you from behind. Second, you can't actually see the transit of Venus through dark glasses or with the naked eye, so the only option was to watch on screen or peer through one of the many telescopes available on site. The programme of talks and events made up for the disappointment, but I did find myself thinking: nearly forty hours in a plane for this?

What really surprised me, though, was contemporary New Zealand nationhood. New Zealand gives equal recognition to the heritage of the Māori and the European settlers or Pākehā. Biculturalism is an attempt to create a new postmodern identity from the tragedy of colonialism. It was worth every minute of the ridiculously long journey to see such an ambitious model at work.

How strange or familiar was it to be paired with poets from the other side of the world and encounter New Zealand poetry?

Brigitte: Before the trip, I saw contemporary English-language poetry from New Zealand as part of the global English-language poetry scene and Māori poetry as an oral tradition, kept alive as a type of folk memory. In the context of German history, folk memory has a dubious ring to it – the same goes for ethnicity.

Someone like me immediately sees the spectre of racial politics and mass extermination. I actually launched straight into the topic on one of the first mornings we were there, as if the matter could be resolved over fried eggs and toast. Naturally, from the perspectives of Chris, Glenn and Hinemoana, it's a great deal more complicated. All three see themselves – in quite different ways – as independent parts of New Zealand's new or re-established Māori–Pākehā culture.

More to the point, the increasingly event-oriented nature of the literary business draws everyone to the question of how oral our poetry can or should be. The schoolbook orthodoxy of poetry as a purely written form now seems like a historical anomaly. Across the globe, people are developing crossover forms and using different techniques to fuse poetry with sounds, song, dance, rituals and the body. It affects anyone who writes poetry – and of course it influenced our work.

Uwe: We never had communication problems with our New Zealand colleagues. And from experience I didn't expect any. Worldwide, there's an understanding that unites people who devote their lives to poetry, and you can absolutely depend on it. At the same time, the reVERSible coordinator Aurélie Maurin has a knack for putting together the right group – thank you, Aurélie! I've been involved in four major projects now, and all four have been a great success on a personal and a creative level. In the course of the Transit project, we were astonished by how each of us read or performed so differently and how the six of us came together so well on the stage. It was a real surprise to see that musicality and singing are so important to all three New Zealand poets. Chris is a poet, a folk singer and university teacher. Hinemoana is a singer and a poet and teaches creative writing. Glenn is a poet and a doctor. Hinemoana and Glenn work in Māori as well as New Zealand English. This showed up my exclusive focus on the written and spoken word and made me want to reinvigorate my work.

Ulrike: I was surprised to meet three writers who share my emphasis on the aurality of their poems. Hinemoana, my translation partner

for the project, leads a second life as a musician which she hardly seems to separate from her work as a poet. Her aural understanding of poetry is very close to my own, although I'm not a musician. Maybe it's not such a coincidence that all three writers from New Zealand understand poetry as an aural medium. The rhythms of the spoken word and poetry are an important part of Māori culture, which is taken up by contemporary New Zealanders of Māori and non-Māori descent.

On the German side, all three poets have worked as translators outside the framework of the reVERSible project. What do you get from collaborating with a foreign-language poet that you wouldn't get working on the translation alone?

Ulrike: Programmes like reVERSible or the poets-translated-by-poets workshop in Edenkoben give me an opportunity to find out what makes a writer tick and how a poem works: what it sounds like in the original language and in the poet's voice, and how I can recreate it in my own language. Of course, if I don't speak the original language, I rely on an interpreter, and so this kind of programme is essential. But even if I'm collaborating with a poet who writes in English or French, it can be helpful to have a third person, someone who knows the poems in all their nuances and can mediate between us when we reach an impasse because of our different approaches or our vanity. And then it becomes a three-way collaboration. You have to negotiate; you misunderstand each other (and then straighten things out); you're obliged to work under pressure (because the other writer can only stay for a few days); you feel constrained (because someone constantly interferes with what you're doing) – but the end result is often genuinely very close to the original tone and form. For me, that's important: I'm looking to find an equivalent in German for the foreign-language poem, something that a university-trained translator wouldn't come up with – and that doesn't sound like a poem by me.

Uwe: Collaborating on the translation of one of your own poems

is always a process of rethinking and partial rewriting. Nothing stays the same when the poem is embraced by another language. It's especially fascinating in the case of English, a language that's supposedly close to German and operates like a universal Latin for the modern age. The task of finding a form for the poem and giving it shape in another language isn't just an exercise in consulting your own word pool to find the right synonym: it takes everything you have as a poet. If you're not prepared to commit your whole self to the process, it's better to not start.

Brigitte: I wouldn't have achieved the same sharpness if I'd worked only from the printed page without meeting the poets and talking to them in situ. This workshop differs from previous reVERSible projects in that we've had more time together and we're writing about a shared experience: the transit of Venus. It's been incredibly productive. It also stands out from previous workshops insofar as we're translating from and into English. On the German side, there's been no need for interpreters or line-by-line translations. At the same time, we're dealing with different degrees of bilingualism, including broken English and classroom German. Then there's te reo Māori, which plays an important role in New Zealand English. Tackling all that over email and Skype would never have worked if we hadn't first spent time with one another in New Zealand. Chris and I had enough trouble with the tried and tested method of the postcard – not to mention the gremlin that gobbled half our emails before we could read them. It's a huge relief that we'll see each other in Berlin this September so that we can finish our work in real time.

Where can I find the South?

Brigitte: Let me quote from a post I wrote for the Frankfurt Book Fair's German-language blog, 'Down Under':

> After thirty-six hours of flying, we're down under and upside down, wide asleep in our jet lag. Straight from summer to winter, which at the top of the North Island is relatively warm. In the South Island it's snowing already.

Northness, as I heard later in a New Zealand poem, means humid dreams of the turquoise Pacific. When southerlies are forecast, you'll need your hat, scarf and gloves.

Ulrike: I've published three collections of poetry, and in one way or another they're all about the South. In the first collection it's there in vague allusions that are unlikely to be recognised by anyone except me. My second collection marked the official announcement of my quest for the South, although I didn't realise it at the time. And in my third collection *Dickicht* I set off in pursuit of the South and finished with an infinity symbol. For me it was never really about a point of the compass: it was more a yearning for an imaginary place that no one can pinpoint on the map, as elusive as the South Pole. My South has much in common with occidental visions of faraway idylls. In the South, happiness, adventure and meaning are found on streets paved with gold: it's what the early theosophers were seeking, and we look for it today in yoga, spa cures, home furnishings and package holidays. The South is the destination you can never reach: as soon as you start travelling towards it, there's another South and it's further away. In *Dickicht* I tried to leave my imaginary journey in the thicket of my language but I didn't reach the end. Having finished the collection, I received the invitation to visit New Zealand, and I felt like a character in one of my own books: no sooner had I arrived than the South moved elsewhere. From the North Island you can fly to Christchurch and take a boat towards Antarctica.

Uwe: My inner compass goes on strike when the sun rises on the wrong side of the sky, the moon doesn't wax as a 'z' and wane as an 'a', and the vast, beautiful, recognisable circumpolar constellations of the northern hemisphere are missing from the sky. It's a question of habit, of course – but the rest of a lifetime couldn't change it. You see: I've taken your request for directions literally.

Translated by Sally-Ann Spencer

Notes

Hinemoana Baker

Some narrative details of 'Songs to Venus I: The Great Flyer' and 'Songs to Venus II: Point of Light' have been adapted from the website UFOInfo: www.ufoinfo.com/humanoid

'Songs to Venus III: Kaikouri Lights' refers to the 'Kaikoura Lights' UFO sightings of December 1978, notable for being the first such 'lights' captured on film. The poem features some direct quotes and paraphrased speech from a New Zealand television interview with John Cordy, radar operator on the night of the first sighting.

'dismantling the crane' is from my collection *kōiwi kōiwi | bone bone* (Victoria University Press: Wellington, 2010).

The following phrases and words reference and/or quote poems by the German poets who partnered with us in this project:

—'every cent of you making war' (originally 'every cent of them / making war'), 'space station', 'Ginger Bee': Brigitte Oleschinski, tr. Andrew Shields, from *Geisterströmung* (Gedichte mit CD, DuMont, 2004).

—'grass-green ring': Ulrike Almut Sandig, tr. Bradley Schmidt, from *Thicket* (original title *Dickicht*, Schoffling & Co., 2011).

—'insistent songs and icebirds': Uwe Kolbe, 'Sailor's All', from 'Sailor's Home' tr. Mick Standen and Jo Tudor, from the anthology *Sailor's Home*, ed. Yang Lian (Shearsman Books Ltd, 2007).

—the word 'transiteers' was used by journalist Toby Manhire in a blog post for the *NZ Listener* about the Transit of Venus event: www.listener.co.nz/transit-of-venus/transit-of-venus-in-tolaga-bay-the-clouds-part-as-the-anthem-sounds/

—'The light which fell on my newborn body is still alive': This phrase is from a podcast I listen to called *The Mental Illness Happy Hour*. A listener called Anne wrote in from Berlin about her atheism, and how her wonder at the natural world, physics and biology is no less intense simply because she doesn't believe in a deity of any kind. Her full response can be found at www.mentalpod.com/Anne-Atheism

Anmerkungen

Hinemoana Baker

Einige der erzählerischen Details in „Songs an die Venus I: Der große Flieger" und „Songs an die Venus II: Lichtpunkt" stammen aus www. ufoinfo.com/humanoid

„Songs an die Venus III: Kaikoura Lichter" bezieht sich auf die „Kaikoura Lichter" genannten UFO-Sichtungen im Dezember 1978, die als die ersten dieser „Lichter" gelten, die filmisch aufgezeichnet wurden. Das Gedicht beinhaltet einige direkte Zitate und paraphrasierte Aussagen von einem neuseeländischen Fernsehinterview mit John Cordy, dem Radarbeobachter in der Nacht der ersten Sichtung.

„den Kran zu zerlegen" aus *kōiwi kōiwi | bone bone* (Victoria University Press: Wellington, 2010).

Folgende Auszüge/Wörter beziehen sich auf oder sind Zitate von Gedichten der deutschen Lyriker, die am Venustransit-Projekt teilgenommen haben:

—„every cent of you making war" (eigentlich „every cent of them / making war"), „space station", „Ginger Bee": Brigitte Oleschinski, üb. v. Andrew Shields, aus *Geisterströmung* (Gedichte mit CD, DuMont, 2004).

—„grass-green ring": Ulrike Almut Sandig, üb. v. Bradley Schmidt, aus *Thicket* (Originaltitel *Dickicht*, Schöffling & Co., 2011).

—„insistent songs" und „icebirds": Uwe Kolbe, „Sailor's All", üb. v. Mick Standen und Jo Tudor, in der Anthologie *Sailor's Home*, Hrsg. Yang Lian, (Shearsman Books Ltd, 2007).

—Das Wort „transiteers" hatte Toby Manhire in seinem Blogartikel über den Venustransit benutzt: www.listener.co.nz/transit-of-venus/ transit-of-venus-in-tolaga-bay-the-clouds-part-as-the-anthem-sounds/

—„das Licht auf meinem neugeborenen Körper, es ist ja immer noch da": Die Formulierung entstammt einem Podcast *The Mental Illness Happy Hour*. Eine Hörerin aus Berlin namens Anne schrieb über ihren Atheismus, sowie über ihr Staunen angesichts der Natur, der Physik und der Biologie, welches nicht weniger intensiv sei, nur weil sie an keinerlei Gottheiten glaube. Hier der Link zu dem vollständigen Beitrag www.mentalpod.com/Anne-Atheism

Glenn Colquhoun

For me as a New Zealander, the Transit of Venus has always been a motif for interaction between Europe and Polynesia; observing it in 1769 was one of the reasons Captain James Cook first came to the South Pacific. With these poems, I wanted to produce a piece of work for the Frankfurt Book Fair that underscored this and specifically drew on links between New Zealand and Germany. Ernst Dieffenbach was a German naturalist who came to New Zealand in 1839 and left a large body of work about his experiences here.

From 1839 to 1841 Dieffenbach lived in New Zealand and provided reports to William Wakefield on its prospects for settlement. He was the country's first resident scientist. He surveyed the Marlborough Sounds and Wellington. He was the first European to climb Mt Taranaki, boiling water on the summit to estimate its height. He sailed to Northland, then passed by foot in a giant loop from Auckland through the centre of the North Island and back again, keeping a pet weka for much of the way. He spent time in New South Wales and the Chatham Islands and collected and recorded as he went. He coined the term *greywacke* for the rock that forms the backbone of New Zealand. He collected the first sample of the mountain buttercup specific to Taranaki, *Ranunculus nivicola*. He gave his name to the Chatham Island rail, now extinct, *Gallirallus dieffenbachii*. And he completed the second grammar ever written of the Māori language.

For a number of years I worked as a doctor for Te Ati Awa, a tribe on the Kapiti Coast in New Zealand. Dieffenbach had trained as a doctor before undertaking his work as a naturalist and in 1839 he helped to tend the wounded at the battle of Kāititanga – which involved this tribe. It occurred to me that he would have treated some of the ancestors of patients I had treated in the past and I wanted to explore this connection between us as well.

These poems are not really written for the page. They are oral poems and exist most fully as sung or chanted poems. I wanted to make the point to a European audience that New Zealand poetry has both a written form as well as an extant oral tradition that is still actively composed in. Each poem is also used as a surface decoration for a gourd or calabash. Gourds were used in the past by Māori as containers, musical instruments and

Glenn Colquhoun

Als Neuseeländer habe ich den Venustransit immer schon als Anlass für den Austausch zwischen Europa und Polynesien gesehen. Unter anderem um dieses Ereignis 1769 zu beobachten, war Kapitän James Cook seinerzeit in den Südpazifik aufgebrochen. Mit diesen Gedichten wollte ich ein Werk für die Frankfurter Buchmesse schaffen, das genau diesen Zusammenhang betont und an die Verbindungen zwischen Neuseeland und Deutschland anknüpft. Ernst Dieffenbach war ein deutscher Naturforscher, der 1839 nach Neuseeland kam und ein umfangreiches Werk über seine Erfahrungen hier hinterließ.

Er lebte zwischen 1839 und 1841 in Neuseeland und verfasste dort Berichte für William Wakefield über die Möglichkeiten einer Besiedlung. Dieffenbach war der erste im Lande ansässige Forscher. Er erkundete die Marlborough Sounds und Wellington. Er war der erste Europäer, der den Mount Taranaki bestieg und auf der Bergspitze mittels des Aufkochens von Wasser versuchte, dessen Höhe zu bestimmen. Er segelte nach Northland, wanderte dann in einem großen Kreis zu Fuß von Auckland durch das Zentrum der Nordinsel und zurück, und wurde für den Großteil seiner Wanderung von einer zahmen Weka-Ralle begleitet. Er verbrachte einige Zeit in New South Wales und auf den Chatham-Inseln, sammelte und notierte auch dort seine Beobachtungen. Er gab den Felsen, die das Rückgrat Neuseelands bilden, ihren Namen, *greywacke*. Er sammelte das erste Exemplar eines Mountain Buttercup, *Ranunculus nivicola*, einem Hahnenfußgewächs, das nur in Taranaki wächst. Er gab auch der Chatham Island Ralle, die heute ausgestorben ist, seinen Namen, *Gallirallus dieffenbachia*. Darüber hinaus erarbeitete er die zweite Sprachlehre über die Sprache der Māori.

Ich arbeitete für einige Jahre als Arzt für Te Ati Awa, einen Stamm an der Kapiti Coast in Neuseeland. Dieffenbach hatte Medizin studiert, bevor er seine Arbeit als Naturforscher aufnahm, und 1839 half er, die Verwundeten der Kāititanga Schlacht – an der jener Stamm beteiligt war zu versorgen. Mir kam in den Sinn, dass er einige der Vorfahren der Patienten behandelt haben dürfte, die ich selbst in der Vergangenheit behandelt hatte. Und auch diese Verbindung zwischen uns wollte ich weiter untersuchen.

Diese Gedichte sind nicht wirklich für die schriftliche Form gedacht. Es sind Sprech-Gedichte und sie kommen gesungen oder

vessels to hold incantations, and were often decorated. Māori art forms such as carving, tukutuku and kōwhaiwhai were elaborate ways of recording stories and were symbol-based. In many ways they were similar to writing and often used to decorate everyday objects.

Above all else, the poems have a specific purpose based on the Māori custom of the kawe mate (the carrying of the dead). This custom involves returning the spirit of a person to the place where they belong after they have died, particularly if that person has been important to a specific people. The gourds and the songs they contain are a way of creating a tangible memorial to Dieffenbach that can be returned to his people. The gourds have now found a home at the Rautenstrauch-Joest-Museum of World Cultures in Cologne, where a large collection of Dieffenbach memorabilia is held. The poems will appear (in English and Māori) in my collection *Myths and Legends of the Ancient Pākehā*.

Chris Price

'Poedua': Poedua [Poetua] was a Society Islands princess painted by John Webber, the ship's artist on Captain Cook's third and final expedition during 1776–1780, the one on which he lost his life. (This was not the same expedition on which Cook was sent to observe the Transit of Venus.) She and her husband were briefly abducted by Cook to use in exchange for two of his crew members, who had deserted. Te Papa's webpage on the painting describes it as 'the first great portrait of an indigenous woman of the South Pacific presented to a European audience.' When some of the Transit poets visited the Te Papa exhibition where the painting was on display, I was struck by the rather English face the artist had given this Polynesian princess, which seemed emblematic of the difficulty many European visitors to the Pacific had in seeing past their own cultural preconceptions at that time. The poem gestures towards some of these divergent perceptions of reality, while being uncomfortably aware that putting words in Poetua's mouth could be seen as just another moment of cultural misrepresentation. I have also given Poetua a bead that does not appear in the painting. A blue glass bead was given to an Uawa woman by one of Cook's crew, and in the play about the first contact between the local people and Cook's scientists and crew devised and performed by students of the Tolaga Bay

skandiert am besten zur Geltung. Ich wollte dem europäischen Publikum deutlich machen, dass Neuseelands Lyrik beides beinhaltet: eine schriftliche aber auch eine noch immer lebendige mündliche Tradition, die nach wie vor genutzt wird. Jedes Gedicht dient auch zur Verzierung der Oberfläche eines Flaschenkürbisses oder Kalebasse. Früher verwendeten die Māori solche Kürbisse, häufig kunstvoll verziert, als Behälter, Musikinstrumente oder Gefäße für Beschwörungen. Kunstformen der Māori, wie Schnitzereien, tukutuku oder kōwhaiwhai waren kunstvolle, symbolhafte Ausdrucksformen, um Geschichten aufzuzeichnen. In vielerlei Hinsicht waren sie ähnlich zur Schrift und dienten oftmals zur Verzierung von Alltagsgegenständen.

Zu allem anderen aber haben die Gedichte auch den auf der Māori-Tradition beruhenden besonderen Zweck des kawe mate (das Überführung der Verstorbenen). Dieser Brauch beinhaltet, den Geist eines Verstorbenen an den Ort heimzuführen, an den er gehört, insbesondere falls der Verstorbene für bestimmte Menschen dort eine große Bedeutung hatte. Die Kürbisse und die Lieder, die sie beinhalten, sind ein Weg, Dieffenbach ein greifbares Andenken zu schaffen, das zu seinem Volk zurückgeführt werden kann. Die verzierten Kürbisse haben nun ein Zuhause gefunden: im Rautenstrauch-Joest-Museum der Kulturen der Welt in Köln, das eine umfassende Sammlung von Dieffenbach-Memorabilia besitzt. Die Gedichte erscheinen 2016 (in Englisch und Māori) in meiner Sammlung *Myths and Legends of the Ancient Pākehā*.

Chris Price

„Poedua": Poedua [Poetua] war eine Prinzessin von den Gesellschaftsinseln. Sie wurde von John Webber porträtiert, dem Schiffskünstler auf der dritten und letzten Expedition Kapitän Cooks zwischen 1776 und 1780, derjenigen, auf der er sein Leben verlor. (Dies war nicht dieselbe Expedition, auf der Cook ausgesandt wurde, um den Venustransit zu beobachten.) Poetua und ihr Ehemann wurden von Cook kurzzeitig verschleppt, um zwei Mitglieder der Schiffsmannschaft zu ersetzen, die desertiert waren. Das Te Papa beschreibt das Gemälde auf seiner Webseite als „das erste große Porträt einer indigenen Frau aus dem Südpazifik, das einem europäischen Publikum präsentiert wurde." Als

Area School on the day of the 2012 Transit, one of the performers wore just such a bead.

'Parallax': Early observers of the Transit encountered a phenomenon that became known as the 'black drop'. At the moment when Venus first appeared to contact the disk of the sun, it sometimes appeared to elongate into a black drop, making the precise start time of the Transit difficult to determine. The 'circle of least confusion' was what the observers hoped to record.

'It is good to speak the language of New Zealand' is a found poem. The source is *A Korao no New Zealand; or, the New Zealander's First Book, Being an Attempt to compose some Lessons for the Instruction of the Natives* (G. Howe, 1815), reproduced in *Words Between Us – He Kōrero: First Māori–Pākehā Conversations on Paper* by Alison Jones and Kuni Jenkins (Huia Publishing, 2011).

'Antipodean': The mentions of 'Krone' and 'terror cove' allude to that fact that the photographer Hermann Krone (1827–1916) took part in a German expedition to observe the 1874 Transit of Venus from Terror Cove in the Auckland Islands. Some of Krone's photographs were displayed in the Adam Art Gallery's *Dark Sky* exhibition, 2012.

einige der „Transit of Venus"- Lyriker die Te Papa Ausstellung besuchten, in der das Gemälde gezeigt wurde, fiel mir doch gleich das eher englische Gesicht auf, mit welchem der Künstler die polynesische Prinzessin versehen hatte. Es schien die Schwierigkeit zu versinnbildlichen, die viele europäische Besucher im Pazifik damit hatten, über die eigenen, vorgefassten kulturellen Vorstellungen dieser Zeit hinauszublicken. Das Gedicht verweist auf einige dieser divergierenden Wahrnehmungen von Wirklichkeit, wobei ich mir dessen bewusst bin, dass Poetua Worte in den Mund zu legen, ebenfalls als eine kulturelle Fehldarstellung betrachtet werden könnte. Ich habe außerdem Poetua mit einer Perle versehen, die nicht in dem Gemälde zu sehen ist. Jemand aus Cooks Mannschaft gab einer Uawa-Frau eine blaue Glasperle, und in dem Theaterstück über das erste Zusammentreffen zwischen den Einheimischen und Cooks Forschern und Mannschaft, aufgeführt von den Schülern der Tolaga Bay Schule am Tag des Venustransit 2012, trug einer der Schauspieler genau solch eine Perle.

„Parallax": Frühe Beobachter des Transits stießen auf ein Phänomen, das später als 'Tropfenphänomen' bekannt wurde. In dem Moment, wenn die Venus gerade die Sonnenscheibe berührt, scheint es manchmal, als würde sich dazwischen ein schmaler, schwarzer Tränentropfen bilden, was es erschwert, den exakten Beginn des Transits zu bestimmen. Die Beobachter hofften den „Kreis der geringsten Zerstreuung" aufzuzeichnen.

„It is good to speak the language of New Zealand" ist ein *found poem*. Die Quelle ist *A Korao no New Zealand; or, the New Zealander's First Book, Being an Attempt to compose some Lessons for the Instruction of the Natives* (G. Howe, 1815), reproduced in *Words Between Us – He Kōrero: First Māori–Pākehā Conversations on Paper* von Alison Jones und Kuni Jenkins (Huia Publishing, 2011).

„Antipodean": Die Erwähnung von „Krone" und der „Terror Cove" spielen darauf an, dass der Fotograf Hermann Krone (1827–1916) an einer deutschen Expedition teilnahm, um den Venustransit 1874 von der Terror-Bucht auf den Auckland-Inseln aus zu beobachten. Einige von Krones Fotografien wurden 2012 in der *Dark Sky* Ausstellung der Adam Art Galerie gezeigt.

About the writers

Hinemoana Baker

Hinemoana Baker's first collection of poetry, *mātuhi | needle*, was published in 2004 in New Zealand and the US. Her second book, *kōiwi kōiwi | bone bone*, was published in 2010 and her third, *waha | mouth* in 2014. Baker studied Māori as an adult and her love for the Māori language, as well as other aspects of her mixed Māori and Pākehā heritage, come through in her poetry. Her work unites observations and experiences of childhood, family, emerging sexuality, politics and culture. Hinemoana has produced albums of her original music and poetry, and has edited several anthologies of New Zealand poetry. She has performed, read and undertaken writers' residencies both in New Zealand and abroad, including a year as Creative New Zealand Berlin Writer in Residence 2015–16. Along with writing, singing and producing, she works as an editor and teacher. For more information, visit www.hinemoana.co.nz.

Ulrike Almut Sandig

Ulrike Almut Sandig was born in Großenhain (GDR) in 1979 and now lives with her family in Berlin. She started publishing her poetry by pasting poems to lamp posts in Leipzig and spreading them on flyers and free post cards. After completing her MA in Religious Studies and Modern Indology, she subsequently graduated from the German Creative Writing Program Leipzig. Two prose books and three volumes of her poetry have been published to date. Previous publications include radio plays and audio-books of poetry and pop music. For her spoken word performances she works with various composers and musicians. In 2009 she was awarded the Leonce and Lena Prize. She has received numerous other awards and scholarships, most recently a scholarship from the Berlin Senate in 2014. In December 2015, Ugly Duckling Presse (Brooklyn, USA) published a selection of her early poems, translated by Bradley Schmidt.

Über die AutorenInnen

Hinemoana Baker

Hinemoana Bakers erste Gedichtsammlung *mātuhi | needle* wurde im Jahr 2004 in Neuseeland und den USA veröffentlicht. Die beiden Bücher *kōiwi kōiwi | bone bone* und *waha | mouth* folgten 2010 und 2014. Im Erwachsenenalter fing Baker an, Māori zu lernen und ihre Leidenschaft für die Māorische Sprache, sowie andere Aspekte ihrer Māori- und Pākehā Abstammung finden sich in ihren Gedichten wieder. Bakers Texte vereinen Beobachtungen und Erfahrungen der Kindheit, Familie, erwachende Sexualität, Politik und Kultur. Baker hat Alben ihrer eigenen traditionellen Musik und Poesie produziert und mehrere Sammelbände über neuseeländische Dichtung herausgegeben. Sie ist in Neuseeland und im Ausland als Lyrikerin und Sängerin aufgetreten und hat an Residenzprogrammen teilgenommen. Für 2015/2016 wurde sie für die Autorenresidenz von Creative New Zealand in Berlin ausgewählt. Neben ihrer Arbeit als Autorin, Sängerin und Produzentin ist sie als Redakteurin und Dozentin tätig. Mehr Informationen unter www.hinemoana.co.nz.

Ulrike Almut Sandig

Ulrike Almut Sandig, 1979 in Großenhain (Sachsen) geboren, lebt mit ihrer Familie in Berlin. Ihre ersten literarischen Texte veröffentlichte sie in Form von Plakaten (Augenpost) an Laternenmasten, Flyern und kostenlosen Postkarten. In Leipzig schloss sie ein Magisterstudium der Religionswissenschaft und modernen Indologie ab, außerdem ein Diplomstudium am Deutschen Literaturinstitut. Bisher erschienen drei Gedichtsammlungen, zwei Erzählbände, zwei popmusikalische Hörbücher (mit Marlen Pelny) und verschiedene Hörspiele. Für ihre Sprechperformances arbeitet sie mit verschiedenen Komponisten und Musikern zusammen. Ihre Gedichte wurden vielfach verfilmt und ausgezeichnet, unter anderem mit dem Leonce-und-Lena-Preis 2009. Auch für ihre Prosa erhielt sie zahlreiche Preise und Stipendien, zuletzt

Glenn Colquhoun

Glenn Colquhoun is a poet and children's writer. His first poetry collection, *The art of walking upright*, won the Jessie Mackay Best First Book of Poetry prize at the 2000 Montana New Zealand Book Awards. *Playing God*, his third collection, won the poetry section of the same awards in 2003 as well as the Reader's Choice Award that year. He has written four children's books and published a book of essays, *Jumping ship and other essays*. He was awarded the Prize in Modern Letters in 2004 and a Fulbright scholarship to Harvard University in 2010. In 2014 he represented New Zealand on the Commonwealth Poets United poetry project which celebrated the Glasgow Commonwealth Games that year. He works as a GP in Horowhenua.

Uwe Kolbe

Uwe Kolbe was born in East Berlin in 1957. His first book, *Hineingeboren* (*Born into*), was published in 1980. He has worked as a translator of Federico García Lorca, among other writers. As co-editor of the magazine *Mikado*, he was able to circumvent a three-year publication ban and continue to publish his own works. In 1985 Uwe travelled in Western Europe and was a visiting lecturer at universities in Vienna and Austin, Texas. He moved to West Germany in 1987. Between 1997 and 2004 he taught creative writing as head of the studio of literature and theatre at the University of Tübingen. He has received many prizes and awards, most recently the Heinrich Mann Prize from the Academy of the Arts in Berlin, and the Meran Poetry Award, both in 2012. A sequence of poems titled *Transit* is included in his most recent collection, Gegenreden (S. Fischer Verlag Frankfurt am Main, 2015); most of these poems were written in New Zealand. He lives in Hamburg.

das Autorenstipendium des Berliner Senats 2014. Im Dezember 2015 veröffentlichte Ugly Duckling Presse (Brooklyn, USA) eine Auswahl ihrer frühen Gedichte, die von Bradley Schmidt übersetzt wurden.

Glenn Colquhoun

Glenn Colquhoun ist Dichter und Kinderbuchautor. Seine erste Gedichtsammlung, *The art of walking upright*, wurde 2000 bei den Montana New Zealand Book Awards mit dem Jessie Mackay Best First Book of Poetry ausgezeichnet. *Playing God*, sein drittes Werk, gewann den gleichen Preis im Jahr 2003 sowie den Readers' Choice Award im selben Jahr. Er veröffentlichte vier Kinderbücher und eine Essaysammlung, *Jumping ship and other essays*. 2004 wurde ihm der Price in Modern Letters der Victoria Universität in Wellington verliehen und 2010 erhielt er ein Fulbright Stipendium für die Harvard Universität. 2014 repräsentierte er Neuseeland beim Commonwealth Poets United-Projekt im Rahmen der Commonwealth Games in Glasgow. Er arbeitet als Allgemeinmediziner in Horowhenua.

Uwe Kolbe

Uwe Kolbe wurde 1957 in Ostberlin geboren. Sein erstes Buch, *Hineingeboren*, erschien 1980 als erster von drei Gedichtbänden im Aufbau-Verlag Berlin/DDR. Seinen Lebensunterhalt bestritt er v. a. mit Nachdichtungen und Übersetzungen, darunter von Theaterstücken des Spaniers García Lorca. Von 1983 bis 1987 war er Mitherausgeber der Untergrundzeitschrift *Mikado*. Ab 1985 genehmigten die Behörden ihm Reisen nach Westdeutschland und Westeuropa. Gastdozenturen führten ihn nach Austin, Texas und Wien. 1987 zog er nach Westdeutschland. Unter den Literaturpreisen, die er für sein Werk erhielt, waren zuletzt der Heinrich-Mann-Preis der Berliner Akademie der Künste sowie der Lyrikpreis Meran, beide 2012. Von 1997 bis 2004 unterrichtete Kolbe Kreatives Schreiben als Leiter des Studio Literatur und Theater der Universität Tübingen. Eine Reihe von Gedichten unter dem Titel *Transit* ist enthalten in seinem jüngsten Gedichtband, *Gegenreden* (S. Fischer Verlag Frankfurt am Main, 2015), die meisten davon entstanden in Neuseeland. Heute lebt er in Hamburg.

Brigitte Oleschinski

Brigitte Oleschinski was born in Cologne in 1955. A critically acclaimed poet, essayist and performer, she trained as an academic historian and political scientist and has a doctorate in twentieth-century German history. She has been invited to international poetry festivals around the world and translates poetry from over a dozen languages. She also gives lectures and workshops on various topics dealing with literature and intercultural dialogue in times of globalisation. She is best known for her poetry collections *Mental Heat Control* (Rowohlt, 1990), *Your Passport is Not Guilty* (Rowohlt, 1997) and *Geisterströmung* (DuMont, 2004). She received the prestigious Peter-Huchel-Preis in 1998. Her other awards include the Ernst-Meister-Preis (2002) and the Austrian Erich-Fried Preis (2004). She lives in Berlin as a freelance writer.

Chris Price

Chris Price's poetry collections include *Husk* (Best First Book of Poetry, New Zealand Book Awards, 2002), *The Blind Singer* (2009) and *Beside Herself* (2016). She has also published an eccentric biographical dictionary that samples the lives of both real and fictional characters called *Brief Lives* (2006), and contributed to the science-art anthology *Are Angels OK?* (2006). Chris was editor of the literary journal *Landfall* for much of the 1990s, and worked as coordinator of Writers and Readers Week for the New Zealand International Arts Festival for over a decade. In 2011 she was awarded the prestigious New Zealand Post Mansfield Prize, which allows a New Zealand writer to live and work for six months in Menton, France. Chris teaches creative writing at the International Institute of Modern Letters, Victoria University of Wellington.

Brigitte Oleschinski

Brigitte Oleschinski wurde 1955 in Köln geboren. Sie gilt als bekannteund erfolgreiche Dichterin, Essayistin und Performerin. Nach einemStudium der Politikwissenschaft arbeitete sie als promovierte Zeithistorikerin zu Fragen der politischen Repression in totalitären Systemen des 20. Jahrhunderts. Sie wurde zu Literaturfestivals auf derganzen Welt eingeladen und hat Gedichte aus mehr als einem Dutzend Sprachen übersetzt, hält Vorlesungen und gibt Workshops, die sich mit Literatur und interkulturellem Dialog in Zeiten der Globalisierungbefassen. Am bekanntesten sind ihre Gedichtbände *Mental Heat Control* (Rowohlt, 1990), *Your Passport is Not Guilty* (Rowohlt, 1997) und *Geisterströmung* (DuMont, 2004). Ihr Werk wurde vielfach ausgezeichnet, darunter 1998 mit dem Peter-Huchel-Preis, 2002 mit dem Ernst-Meister-Preis und 2004 mit dem Erich-Fried-Preis. Brigitte Oleschinski lebt als freie Schriftstellerin in Berlin.

Chris Price

Zu Chris Price Werken gehören *Husk* (Bester erster Gedichtband, New Zealand Book Awards, 2002), *The Blind Singer* (2009) und *Beside Herself* (2016). Sie hat ein Exzentrisches Biografisches Wörterbuch veröffentlicht, das das Leben von realen wie fiktiven Charakteren unter die Lupe nimmt (*Brief Lives*, 2006), und an dem Kunst- und Wissenschafts-Sammelband *Are Angels OK?* (2006) mitgewirkt. In den 1990 ern war sie Redakteurin für das Literaturmagazin *Landfall* und über zehn Jahre lang koordinierte sie die Writers and Readers Week für das New Zealand International Arts Festival. 2011 wurde ihr der angesehene New Zealand Post Mansfield Preis verliehen, der es neuseeländischen Autoren ermöglich, für sechs Monate in Menton, Frankreich zu leben und zu arbeiten. Derzeit lehrt Chris Kreatives Schreiben am International Institute of Modern Letters an der Victoria Universität in Wellington.

Acknowledgements

The Transit of Venus Poetry Exchange was organised by the Goethe-Institut New Zealand, the International Institute of Modern Letters, and the Literaturwerkstatt Berlin, and was supported by the German Federal Foreign Office, the New Zealand government through Manatū Taonga – the New Zealand Ministry for Culture and Heritage's Cultural Diplomacy International Programme, and the Publishers Association of New Zealand. The Transit of Venus Forum and associated events were put together in partnership between the MacDiarmid Institute, Victoria University of Wellington, and Te Aitanga-a-Hauiti. The eco-restoration project is a collaboration between Te Aitanga-a-Hauiti, the local community and the Allan Wilson Centre for Molecular Ecology and Evolution.

The poets' heartfelt thanks go to the following people and organisations:
Germany: Aurélie Maurin, Christiane Lange, Thomas Wohlfahrt, and Heiko Strunk of the Literaturwerkstatt Berlin; our interlinear translators Bradley Schmidt, Donna Stonecipher and Catherine Hales; the Museum für Völkerkunde, Hamburg; the Rautenstrauch-Joest-Museum of World Cultures, Cologne; the Frankfurt Book Fair; *Die Horen* magazine, where the interview with the German poets first appeared; and Sally-Ann Spencer for the English translation of the interview. Hinemoana Baker thanks Kate Camp, whose hospitality, company and advice were very much appreciated from Berlin to Frankfurt.

New Zealand: Goethe-Institut New Zealand Director Bettina Senff and Ulrike Rosenfeld; Bill Manhire (International Institute of Modern Letters); the people of Uawa / Tolaga Bay, especially the extraordinary students and teachers of the Uawa / Tolaga Bay Area School; the MacDiarmid Institute and Te Aitanga-a-Hauiti; Sarah Ropata and Linda Halle of the NZ@Frankfurt team; Geoffrey Batchen and Christina Barton of the Adam Art Gallery, for the *Dark Sky* exhibition that inspired a number of these poems; Rhonda Paku, Matiu Baker and Sean Mallon for a front- and back-of-house view of collections and exhibitions at Te Papa Tongarewa, and Ashleigh Young.

Danksagungen

Der Transit of Venus Poetry Exchange wurde von folgenden Projektpartnern organisiert: Goethe-Institut Neuseeland, International Institute of Modern Letters, Literaturwerkstatt Berlin. Das Projekt wurde weiterhin von folgenden Organisationen unterstützt: durch das Auswärtige Amt Deutschlands, von der neuseeländischen Regierung durch das Manatū Taonga Programm für internationale kulturelle Diplomatie des neuseeländischen Ministeriums für Kultur und Nationales Erbe und durch den neuseeländischen Verlegerverband. Das Transit of Venus Forum und die damit verbundenen Veranstaltungen wurden in Zusammenarbeit von dem MacDiarmid Institute, der Victoria University of Wellington und Te Aitanga-a-Hauiti organisiert. Das Öko-Restaurations-Projekt ist eine Kooperation von Te Aitanga-a-Hauiti, der lokalen Gemeinde und dem Allan Wilson Zentrum für Molekulare Ökologie und Evolution.

Die Lyriker danken herzlich den folgenden Personen und Organisationen:
Deutschland: Aurélie Maurin, Christiane Lange, Thomas Wohlfahrt und Heiko Strunk, Literaturwerkstatt Berlin; den interlinearen Übersetzern Bradley Schmidt, Donna Stonecipher und Catherine Hales; dem Museum für Völkerkunde, Hamburg; dem Rautenstrauch-Joest-Museum-Kulturen der Welt, Köln; der Frankfurter Buchmesse; Die Horen Magazin, in dem die Interviews mit den deutschen Lyrikerinnen und Lyrikern als erstes erschienen; und Sally-Ann Spencer für die englische Übersetzung des Interviews. Hinemoana Baker dankt Kate Camp, deren Gastfreundschaft, Begleitung und Ratschläge von Berlin nach Frankfurt sehr wertgeschätzt wurden.

Neuseeland: Goethe-Institut Neuseeland, der Institutsleiterin Bettina Senff und Ulrike Rosenfeld; Bill Manhire (International Institute of Modern Letters); den Menschen von Uawa / Tolaga Bay, insbesondere den außergewöhnlichen Studierenden und Lehrenden der Uawa / Tolaga Bay Bezirksschule; dem MacDiarmid Institut und Te Aitanga-a-Hauiti; Sarah Ropata und Linda Halle des NZ@Frankfurt Teams; Geoffrey Batchen und Christina Barton der Adam Art Galerie, für die *Dark Sky* Ausstellung,

Epigraphs

The whakataukī (proverb) comes from a speech by Māori Party MP Te Ururoa Flavell at the First Reading of the Waka Umanga (Māori Corporations) Bill on 11 December 2007. See Parliamentary Debates (Hansard), Volume 644, page 13867.

'Wie schön leucht' uns der Morgenstern' ['How bright appears the morning star']: Philipp Nicolai, 1597

'Christmas' by Bill Manhire originally appeared in the December 2014 issue of *Poetry* magazine.

Images

Cover: 'Venus transit, clouds, 2004', Wolfgang Tillmans, reproduced courtesy of the artist

Transit of Venus Poetry Exchange photographs (pp. 12, 55, 119): Ulrike Rosenfeld / Goethe-Institut New Zealand

Telescope (p. 100): Linda Halle

Gourds (p. 48): Kathrin Simon

New Zealand Pavilion at the 2012 Frankfurt Book Fair (pp. 6, 66): NZ@Frankfurt, photographs by Lisa Gardiner, Manatū Taonga

Postcards (p. 97): Postcards of images from the *Dark Sky* exhibition (Adam Art Gallery, 2012)

Transiteers, left to right (p. 119): Ulrike Almut Sandig, Brigitte Oleschinksi, Uwe Kolbe

Elsewhere

A short film about the Transit of Venus Poetry Exchange: www.youtube.com/watch?v=l7wb7C1IDrw

Print and audio versions of some of the poems in this book can be found at www.lyrikline.org along with other work by the poets.

Two audio tracks by Ulrike Almut Sandig: www.ulrike-almut-sandig.de/audiothek/ (See 'Hörstücke'.)

An account of the Transit of Venus Forum at Tolaga Bay: www.royalsociety.org.nz/events/2012-transit-of-venus-forum-lifting-our-horizon/forum-programme/

die eine Reihe dieser Gedichte inspiriert hat; Rhonda Paku, Matiu Baker und Sean Mallon für eine Führung durch die Sammlungen und Ausstellungen im Te Papa Tongarewa, und Ashleigh Young.

Inschriften

Das Whakataukī (Sprichwort) stammt aus einer Rede der Māori Partei MP Te Ururoa Flavell während der Ersten Lesung der Waka Umanga (Māori Corporation) Charta am 11. Dezember 2007. Siehe dazu die Parlamentsdebatte (Hansard), Band 644, Seite 13867.

'Wie schön leucht' uns der Morgenstern': Philipp Nicolai, 1597

„Christmas" von Bill Manhire erschien ursprünglich in der Dezember 2014 Ausgabe des *Poetry* Magazins.

Bilder

Deckblatt: „Venus transit, clouds, 2004", Wolfgang Tillmans

Transit of Venus Poetry Exchange Fotografien (S. 12, 55, 119): Ulrike Rosenfeld / Goethe-Institut Neuseeland

Teleskop (S. 100): Linda Halle

Bemalte Kürbisse (S. 48): Kathrin Simon

Neuseeland-Pavillon auf der Frankfurter Buchmesse 2012 (S. 6, 66): NZ@Frankfurt, Fotografien von Lisa Gardiner, Manatū Taonga

Postkarten (p. 97): Postkarten von Bildern aus der *Dark Sky* Ausstellung (Adam Art Gallery, 2012)

Transiteers, links nach rechts (S. 119): Ulrike Almut Sandig, Brigitte Oleschinksi, Uwe Kolbe

Sonstiges

Ein Kurzfilm über den Transit of Venus Poetry Exchange: www.youtube.com/watch?v=l7wb7C1IDrw

Druck- und Hörfassungen von einigen der Gedichte in diesem Buch sind auf www.lyrikline.org, zusammen mit anderen Werken der Lyriker zu finden.

Zwei Aufnahmen von Ulrike Almut Sandig: www.ulrike-almut-sandig.de/audiothek/ (Siehe „Hörstücke".)

Ein Bericht des Transit of Venus Forums in Tolaga Bay: www.royalsociety.org.nz/events/2012-transit-of-venus-forum-liftingourhorizon/forum-programme

Transit of Venus Poetry Exchange organised by

INTERNATIONAL INSTITUTE
OF MODERN LETTERS
Te Pūtahi Tuhi Auaha o te Ao

Supported by